Tender Mercies

Prayers for Healing and Coping

By Mary Peter Martin, FSP

Pauline
BOOKS & MEDIA
Boston

Nihil Obstat: Reverend Vincent Daily, S.T.D.
Imprimatur: ✠ Seán Cardinal O'Malley, O.F.M. Cap.
  Archbishop of Boston
February 2, 2007

Library of Congress Cataloging-in-Publication Data

Martin, Mary Peter.
  Tender mercies : prayers for healing and coping / by Mary Peter Martin.
    p. cm.
  Includes bibliographical references and index.
    ISBN 0-8198-7424-8 (pbk. : alk. paper) 1. Consolation. 2. Suffering—Religious
aspects—Christianity. 3. Prayers. I. Title.
  BV4909.M373 2007
  242'.86—dc22

                                2006038015

Cover design by Rosana Usselmann

Cover photo by Mary Emmanuel Alves, FSP

Published by Pauline Books & Media, 50 Saint Paul's Avenue, Boston, MA 02130-3491.
www.pauline.org.

Printed in the U.S.A.

Pauline Books & Media is the publishing house of the Daughters of St. Paul, an international congregation of women religious serving the Church with the communications media.

1 2 3 4 5 6 7 8 9   12 11 10 09 08 07

By the tender mercy of our God,
the dawn from on high will break upon us,
to give light to those who sit
in darkness and in the shadow of death,
to guide our feet into the way of peace.

(Lᴋ 1:78–79)

Contents

Acknowledgments

THANKS ARE DUE to all whose encouragement and honesty were behind this book. A special word of gratitude goes to Dr. Michael St. Clair, teacher, psychologist, and counselor, who first suggested printing these prayer reflections. Thanks to Howie, Marlene, Theresa, Diane, and others whose firsthand experience provided inspiration. A special word of thanks to my fellow Sisters, Daughters of St. Paul, and our associates at Pauline Books & Media, who were involved in the editing and publishing of this work—meant to bring comfort as only prayer can—to those afflicted with anxiety, addiction, mental illness, or who are troubled in spirit.

— Sr. Mary Peter Martin, FSP

Introduction:
Mercy and Comfort

As I stood in the lobby entrance of a Boston hospital, I saw a group of men and women emerge from an inner hallway. Apparently they were taking a break from a group therapy session. My gaze caught the eyes of a young woman named Karen. She ran over to me and implored, "Sister, heal me!" While Karen's mother looked on with grieved dismay, I promised that I would certainly pray for her, but added that I could not heal her—only God can do that. "If only she would smile, just once," her mother said to me as she steered Karen back into the session.

I was still in the lobby when a woman in her thirties, with her car keys jangling, approached me and said, "Sister, pray for me. My son has Tourette's Syndrome. I really need your prayers!" Again I made a promise of prayer. As men and women of all ages and walks of life came and went, I witnessed the struggles of caregivers and care receivers, some afflicted with clinical disorders, others less afflicted but still very anxious. Like Karen, who suffers from a debilitating clinical depression, and her mother, who suffers from the untold stress of a 24/7 caregiver, each person in that lobby carried a burden of anxiety or, at the very least, the weight of family and financial responsibilities.

I had seen intense suffering before that day. As a very young religious Sister in Buffalo, I saw firsthand the suffering of a mother whose 26-year-old son was dying of cancer. Her son's once handsome face was etched deep with pain. She confided to me, "Now I understand and I can feel in myself what Mary went through when she saw her Son dying on the cross." As intense as that mother's sufferings were, they were confined to a relatively short time. Those who feel troubled in spirit or who suffer depression or other emotional stress long to run free. Like Karen's mother, they yearn for the sunshine of a spontaneous and unfettered smile for themselves or for those they love.

Living in Alaska for a few years taught me something about weather and the stark reality of life in extended periods of darkness. On my last stay in Seward, Alaska, it rained for ten of fourteen days. As my Sister companion and I waited for the arctic monsoons to let up, we both were grateful that we had previously experienced the beauty of Alaska's tall pines climbing the rugged hills and mountains, because during that entire trip, the clouds clung to the tree tops and masked the hills from sight. It was as if a stagehand had draped a gray curtain over the landscape.

Anxiety, stress, and depression can shroud our emotional lenses with dark and foggy scenarios in a similar way. Even while the sun of God's grace is trying to blaze through, the fog of our inner heaviness surrounds us like an iron curtain. At times like these we appreciate the comfort and support of others.

WHERE IS GOD WHEN we feel so blue and disoriented? Saint Thérèse of Lisieux—who often experienced spiritual darkness, and even seems to have suffered a nervous breakdown as a teenager—searched for God in the depths of her heart. In her autobiography, *The Story of a Soul,* Thérèse describes her emotional state as "being born and living all the time in a land of fog." Faith taught her that the very Maker of the sunlight walked in the land of fog for thirty-three years to lead us to the light. She described a particular time of spiritual darkness as living in a tunnel. Yet, this saint, despite all her struggle with agonizing darkness, always appeared serene and happy to her fellow Sisters. Somehow, her prayer life served as the lighthouse piercing the darkness of her "land of fog."

Unlike Thérèse, others who suffer are not always able to appear serene. Caregivers, people with emotional and mental disorders, persons under long-term or temporary stress need to reach out for help. Unfortunately, some escape into manic activity; others retreat into a cocoon of sadness and inertia. Still others feel the multiple forms of emotional and mental disquiet. Troubled persons may not feel like praying or pray only as a last resort. Spiritual masters attest that prayer always helps—even if we don't feel its help—because prayer connects us with God, the source of all good.

A retreat director once told me, "Prayer plunges us deep into the presence of God." As I contemplate those words, I visualize a deep sea diver. To survive below the ocean surface, a diver must wear a mask and have a constant oxygen supply. Each time he or she goes into the deep, there is more to see. Prayer is not as complicated as deep sea diving. Yet it is a plunge. The Eternal One who loves us is, as Saint Catherine of Siena said, a Sea of Peace. The more we become persons of prayer, the deeper we are immersed in the Sea of Peace.

I can imagine that Karen (the young woman in my opening story), and perhaps her mother, burdened with stress or suffering from anxiety, might find prayer and the effort to maintain an on-going spirituality tiresome. Certain personalities try hard to become good "pray-ers" but fall into scruples. Instead, a life of balanced prayer wires us, so to speak, for the fulfillment of Jesus' invitation to "come and be refreshed."

In these pages, I offer prayer suggestions for the person who suffers any form of anxiety; for anyone who feels the weight of pressures from work, family life, and failed relationships, or from loss and loneliness; and for caregivers of those suffering from emotional or psychological ills and addictions.

Those who are burdened with anxious thoughts, stress, and compulsions, such as workaholism, may think that prayer is too time-consuming. Or they may be so engrossed in their activities that they cannot find time to talk to God. Even someone with a clinical disorder can take the deep sea dive into the oceans of mercy God offers. At such times, one may seek a "no-pressure" approach to prayer—simply allowing God to admire us, the work of his hands, and in our turn, admiring the One who is the Source of our being.

If we feel that our exterior and interior lives are just too messy for us to pray, we still turn to God, who in the Gospel of Luke is described as a housewife who sweeps vigorously to find a lost coin (see 15:8–10). God's persistent grace can transform our spiritual cottage into a castle.

One who feels beaten by life's hardships, abuse, or addictions may recall the story of the Good Samaritan, who in the Gospel parable found a man beaten and robbed by vicious thieves. The Samaritan hoisted the victim onto his beast and brought him to an inn. Some writers compare the beast—a horse or donkey—to

Christ, who carries us despite the weight of our sins and burdens. When you feel beaten, allow Christ to carry you *and* your burdens.

Other people may know intellectually that God loves them, but their depression makes them feel abandoned. The life of Saint Benedict Joseph Labré offers comfort to those who feel rejected by God. Saint Benedict, a mentally ill, homeless pilgrim, spent his life in works of charity and prayerful adoration. As Blessed Mother Teresa of Calcutta said, "God does not look for our success, but at our effort." The very struggle that one experiences in trying to offer the smallest prayer in the midst of anxiety is a gift to God— and it reassures us that God has not, in fact, rejected us.

Often a person who feels troubled may believe that he or she is not in any shape to approach God in prayer. Troubled memories or the weight of anxiety might cause one to feel incapable of receiving love and affection from God. God, however, is more in love with us than we can possibly love ourselves. Through the prayers offered in this book, may the reader be opened to the flood of God's tender mercies. May these mercies be evident in the gift of peace that God grants to his beloved.

Faith and prayer are like hand and glove. At times both are hard to practice. The prolific short story writer, Flannery O'Connor, shared this great insight about prayer and faith with her friend:

> A faith that just accepts is a child's faith and all right for children, but eventually you have to grow religiously as every other way, though some never do. What people don't realize is how much

religion costs. They think faith is a big electric blanket, when of course, it is the cross.... You must at least do this: keep an open mind. Keep it open toward faith, keep wanting it, keep asking for it, and leave the rest to God.

I don't set myself up to give spiritual advice but all I would like you to know is that I sympathize and I suffer this way myself. When we get our spiritual house in order, we'll be dead. This goes on. You arrive at enough certainty to be able to make your way, but it is making it in the darkness. Don't expect faith to clear up things for you. It is trust, not certainty.[1]

SAINT PAUL WROTE that the Bible, God's word, was written for our instruction as well as for prayer. Both the Hebrew Scripture, commonly called the Old Testament, and the New Testament offer a treasury of prayers, insights, and sound advice. Prayers of praise, of thanksgiving, of sorrow, and of petition are woven into the fabric of both the Old and New Testaments.

The psalms are Bible prayers that can bring us consolation in the midst of the deepest anguish. The psalms were sung in ancient Israel for worship. With the psalms, we use God's word to express our deepest feelings to him. Some of the loveliest and most consoling psalms speak of God's care for us and our desire to return love for love. Jesus prayed the psalms even as he was dying. His cry, "My God, my God, why have you forsaken me?" (Mt 27:46) is taken from Psalm 22. When praying with Scripture, we can pray aloud, or we can pray with our minds and hearts, allowing the Lord to teach, console, and advise us with his word. In the Second Letter to Timothy we are told that Scripture is "useful for teaching, for reproof, for correction, and for training in righteousness" (3:16).

To help focus on God's presence, devout Jews continue the ancient custom of using prayer shawls and attaching to their arms tiny boxes containing lines from the Bible. As Christians, we can dedicate a part of our house, or a corner of our room, as our "prayer shawl space": a reminder that God is truly present in his word and deserves our full attention. God wants to speak to us and with us as a friend.

The psalms also challenge us to express our rage, disappointment, and deepest fears to God. Psalms that call for vengeance on one's enemies may even scare or repel us, proposing an almost war-like treatment of the enemy. We can, however, apply this violence to our spiritual enemies. Bible scholars offer assurance that praying the psalms that call for the punishment of our enemies emboldens our spirits in the face of evil. God is not afraid of our anger or frustrations. Like Tevye in *Fiddler on the Roof,* who told God, "Why don't you pick somebody else?" when he and his fellow Jews were persecuted, we, too, can be completely honest with God, the One who dispels our enemies—or at least helps us cope with them. Some of these enemies are our temptations, laziness, and stubbornness; our lusts, disorders, and, of course, the devil himself. Enemies can take the form of menacing moods, manic activity, or obsessions that drive us without mercy. They may also be our shutting down from social activity, our unwillingness to seek help, or our avoidance of medications prescribed for our good. Our enemies may be lurking in chat rooms or websites on the Internet that glorify disorders even under the guise of support groups. The Bible's Wisdom books direct us to choose our friends wisely, wherever we meet them.

About one-third of the 150 psalms in the Bible are called Psalms of Lament. The writer complains to God; rage and anger boil over. The psalmist objects that God allows—and even seems to be causing—problems in personal and community situations. The Psalms of Lament closely resemble the long list of troubles that afflict people in mind, spirit, and body today. God is not so thin-skinned and accepts these laments as true prayers from the heart. God does not expect us to be repressed and shy. We are to pray, instead, like little children, who are often bold and direct when they ask their parents for what they want.

The psalms stand out as prayers of praise and thanks, anguish, sorrow, and petition. The narrative stories in the Bible are also permeated with prayers. Esther and Judith—women who saved their people from extermination—both provide models of faith and trust in God. Their honest and anguished prayers can serve as a springboard to anyone who feels crushed under the weight of illness, fear, debt, sadness, and any other sorrow that life may bring. Esther faced the reality of a pogrom, a planned genocide of her people, and responded with prayer, fasting, and unshakable trust in the power of God. Both women emerged victorious due to their prayer and courageous action.

Prayers and advice from the Bible are offered in these pages so we may pray with the word of God as we find it in the Sacred Scripture. May these formal prayers, wisdom, encouragement, and directives from the Bible lead us to a greater ease and honesty in our prayer. For most of the psalm prayers offered here in this book, only a portion of the psalm is given. You are invited to open the Bible and pray the entire psalm, or as much of it as you desire.

IN PRAYER, WE SEEK to *praise* God's infinite goodness, especially in creating and upholding us. We seek to *thank* God for all that we receive. We seek to *rejoice* in the mystery of God's love that surrounds us. As we seek God in prayer, we humbly *seek his tender mercies* toward us and ask him to cradle us in his loving care. In prayer, then, let us "cast all our care" upon the One who loves us unconditionally.

A written formula of prayer can be either a steppingstone to wordless prayer or an anchor to grasp amid life's distractions. At times one may be able to pray only a phrase or a single line. When tempted to find excuses not to pray, using a prayer book like this one can help. Devoting precious time to prayer costs us, whether we pride ourselves on our mental health or find ourselves in a clinical state. Often, when we set ourselves to pray, our minds are bombarded with things we have to do. This book offers a variety of prayers for persons who find themselves mentally or emotionally vulnerable, as well as for caregivers and companions. It is my hope that the reader's journey to God will be one of trust, knowing that prayer will bring him or her into living and loving contact with our God who *is* love, mercy, and compassion. Let us begin our prayer.

To Hem in Our Days:
Morning and Evening Prayers

A TAILOR KNOWS that the very last touch on a new garment is the hem. The hem completes it and makes it presentable as well as useful. If we hem in our day with prayer, then things may less easily unravel!

A Morning Psalm

A psalm is a prayer taken from the Bible's own prayer book: the Book of Psalms. These were originally songs or poetic verses expressing praise, thanks, sorrow, and anguished cries to God for help. The word psalm stems from the Greek word psallein, *which means "to pluck" as fingers pluck strings on a harp. Tradition tells us that King David played the harp and wrote some of the psalms.*

Listen to the sound of my cry,
   my King and my God,
   for to you I pray.
O LORD, in the morning you hear my voice;

in the morning I plead my case to you, and watch....
But I, through the abundance of your steadfast love,
   will enter your house,
I will bow down toward your holy temple
   in awe of you.
Lead me, O LORD, in your righteousness
   because of my enemies;
     make your way straight before me....
For you bless the righteous, O LORD;
   you cover them with favor as with a shield.
(Ps 5:2–3, 7–8, 12)

Invitations from the Lord

Between the demands and crises of each day, ask the Lord, "Where are you in the midst of all of this? What are you asking of me?" In the Gospels, Jesus issued several invitations to us. Could one of these be hidden in the hustle and bustle or the monotony of this day?

"The Teacher is here and is calling for you." (Jn 11:28)

He said to them, "Come away to a deserted place all by yourselves and rest a while." (Mk 6:31)

As a carpenter, Jesus may well have fashioned wooden yokes for local farmers. He calls us to share the yoke with him. No matter how stressed we may feel, we are not alone. Jesus is shouldering our load right alongside us.

"Come to me, all you that are weary and are carrying heavy burdens, and I will give you rest. Take my yoke upon you, and learn from me; for I am gentle and humble in heart, and you will find rest for your souls. For my yoke is easy, and my burden is light." (Mt 11:28–30)

Anyone who has competed in a long-distance race or played on a sports team knows in his or her muscles and bones the truth of the saying, "No pain, no gain." The prize we seek to gain outweighs any sacrifice. Self-denial replaces self-gratification; and a focused, disciplined, Christ-centered life leads not to a medal or a trophy, but to life everlasting.

"If any want to become my followers, let them deny themselves and take up their cross and follow me. For those who want to save their life will lose it, and those who lose their life for my sake, and for the sake of the gospel, will save it. For what will it profit them to gain the whole world and forfeit their life? Indeed, what can they give in return for their life?" (Mk 8:34–37)

"Let anyone who is thirsty come to me, and let the one who believes in me drink." (Jn 7:37–38)

"Could you not keep awake one hour? Keep awake and pray that you may not come into the time of trial; the spirit indeed is willing, but the flesh is weak." (Mk 14:37–38)

Jesus' Promises

Many saintly people followed "power ideas," focusing their energies in one direction. Most of these power ideas were Gospel passages. It's a good idea to take some time, before we head into the activity of our day, to read and reflect on one of these promises of Jesus.

If you have ever felt left out, out of place, or just plain lonely, remember that the Father and the Son with the Holy Spirit are waiting to embrace you and dwell in you.

"Everything that the Father gives me will come to me, and anyone who comes to me I will never drive away...." (Jn 6:37)

Life's bruises can make our hearts feel shriveled up. Yet God is working to renew us and give us new hearts on fire with love for God and for others.

"...Let the one who believes in me drink. As the scripture has said, 'Out of the believer's heart shall flow rivers of living water.' Now he said this about the Spirit, which believers in him were to receive." (Jn 7:38–39)

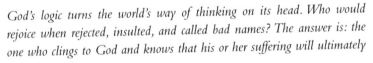

To put forth new life, every seed undergoes a stark transformation. It breaks apart and softens. We too are being transformed from day to day. God works to soften our hard edges. Our hearts are cracked open to make room for God's tenderness.

"Very truly, I tell you, unless a grain of wheat falls into the earth and dies, it remains just a single grain; but if it dies, it bears much fruit. Those who love their life lose it, and those who hate their life in this world will keep it for eternal life. Whoever serves me must follow me, and where I am, there will my servant be also. Whoever serves me, the Father will honor." (Jn 12:24–26)

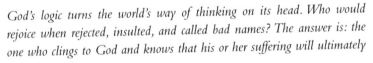

God's logic turns the world's way of thinking on its head. Who would rejoice when rejected, insulted, and called bad names? The answer is: the one who clings to God and knows that his or her suffering will ultimately result in good.

"Blessed are you when people hate you, and when they exclude you, revile you, and defame you on account of the Son of Man. Rejoice in that day and leap for joy, for surely your reward is great in heaven." (Lk 6:22–23)

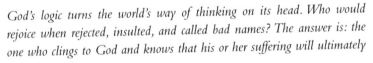

These words about Jesus' resurrection are the rock-solid anchor that sustains us in grief, in anxious moments, and in the face of our own mortality.

Jesus said... "I am the resurrection and the life. Those who believe in me, even though they die, will live, and everyone who lives and believes in me will never die." (Jn 11:25–26)

I once met a young man who had, for a time, stopped going to the celebration of the Eucharist. He said, "Then one day I remembered the words, 'He who eats my flesh and drinks my blood has eternal life.' I want eternal life. That's why I go to Mass every Sunday." Eucharist comes from the Greek word for "thanksgiving." Our Communion makes us persons truly alive in Christ and thankful for the gift of God's life in us.

"Those who eat my flesh and drink my blood have eternal life, and I will raise them up on the last day; for my flesh is true food and my blood is true drink. Those who eat my flesh and drink my blood abide in me, and I in them. Just as the living Father sent me, and I live because of the Father, so whoever eats me will live because of me. This is the bread that came down from heaven, not like that which your ancestors ate, and they died. But the one who eats this bread will live forever." (Jn 6:54–58)

An Evening Psalm

If we feel loaded down with cares and can't sleep, this psalm expresses a great desire that God will set things right for us. The "adversaries" here may be our worries, anxieties, or financial difficulties.

Hear a just cause, O LORD; attend to my cry;
    give ear to my prayer from lips free of deceit.
From you let my vindication come;
    let your eyes see the right.

If you try my heart, if you visit me by night,
    if you test me, you will find no wickedness in me;
    my mouth does not transgress.
As for what others do, by the word of your lips
    I have avoided the ways of the violent.
My steps have held fast to your paths;
    my feet have not slipped.

I call upon you, for you will answer me, O God;
    incline your ear to me, hear my words.
Wondrously show your steadfast love,
    O savior of those who seek refuge
    from their adversaries at your right hand.

Guard me as the apple of the eye;
    hide me in the shadow of your wings.... (Ps 17:1–8)

Take Cover Under God's Wings

Once, on a visit to Johnson Island in the Pacific, I saw frigate birds up close. Just one wing was wide enough to easily shelter all of us in the little boat we were riding. God's "wings" surround us always to protect us. Psalm 91 uses powerful imagery to assure us of God's protection no matter the source of our fears and anxiety. The Church uses this psalm every Sunday for Night Prayer in the Liturgy of the Hours. This vigil prayer begins our week with confidence in God's loving care.

> You who live in the shelter of the Most High,
>   who abide in the shadow of the Almighty,
> will say to the LORD, "My refuge and my fortress;
>   my God, in whom I trust."
> For he will deliver you from the snare of the fowler
>   and from the deadly pestilence;
> he will cover you with his pinions,
>   and under his wings you will find refuge;
>   his faithfulness is a shield and buckler.
> You will not fear the terror of the night,
>   or the arrow that flies by day,
> or the pestilence that stalks in darkness,
>   or the destruction that wastes at noonday. (Ps 91:1–6)

The following lines from this psalm can remind us that our guardian angels are ever on the watch to care for us.

For he will command his angels concerning you
    to guard you in all your ways.
On their hands they will bear you up,
    so that you will not dash your foot against a stone.
You will tread on the lion and the adder,
    the young lion and the serpent you will trample
        under foot.

Those who love me, I will deliver;
    I will protect those who know my name.
When they call to me, I will answer them;
    I will be with them in trouble,
    I will rescue them and honor them. (Ps 91:11–15)

A Prayer for Each Night

For some people, the darkness of approaching night conjures old fears, disturbing memories, and unpleasant dreams. In this prayer we gather the loose ends of our day and offer everything back to God, trusting that he will guard us all night long as restful sleep restores our bodies and souls.

I adore you, my God, and I love you with all my heart. I thank you for loving me into existence, gifting me with Christian life,

and for having cared for me and kept me this day. Please forgive my sins and failings of this day. Accept the good I have done. Take care of me while I sleep. I entrust all my loved ones to your watchful care. I trust that your grace will always be with me and with all my dear ones. Jesus and Mary, I ask your holy blessing on me: In the name of the Father, and of the Son, and of the Holy Spirit. Amen.

Angels and Us

Throughout the story of salvation in the Bible, God sent angels to protect his loved ones. He does the same for us daily.

I am going to send an angel in front of you, to guard you on the way and to bring you to the place that I have prepared. (Ex 23:20)

See, my angel shall go in front of you. (Ex 32:34)

When we cried to the LORD, he heard our voice, and sent an angel. (Num 20:16)

Gideon, a very ordinary person, was chosen and equipped by God to rescue his people from enemy attacks. Through his angels God rescues us, too, from the attacks of our enemies that may wear the guise of stress, anger, fear, addiction, compulsion, or a myriad of other masks.

The angel of the LORD appeared to him and said to him, "The LORD is with you, you mighty warrior." (Judg 6:12)

This is the prayer of Tobit for his son Tobias as he set out to find his future bride, Sarah. Tobit's story assures us that God does surround us with care every day and wants to heal us.

"May God in heaven bring you safely there and return you in good health to me; and may his angel, my son, accompany you both for your safety." (Tob 5:17)

Here the older Tobit assures his wife that their son will return safely because he is in the company of an angel.

"For a good angel will accompany him; his journey will be successful, and he will come back in good health." (Tob 5:22)

When the Maccabees faced the enemies of Israel in battle they prayed like this:

"O Sovereign of the heavens, send a good angel to spread terror and trembling before us." (2 Macc 15:23)

The psalms reassure us of the protection of God's angel.

The angel of the LORD encamps
around those who fear him, and delivers them. (Ps 34:7)

The Letter to the Hebrews reminds us that our good deed to strangers is likened to entertaining angels.

Do not neglect to show hospitality to strangers, for by doing that some have entertained angels without knowing it. (Heb 13:2)

Prayers of Confidence and Comfort

A Prayer to Jesus, My Inmost Counselor

Human counselors have remarkable gifts of listening and offering insight. Yet, these persons cannot see our thoughts, nor probe our inmost hearts. Only Jesus is the ultimate counselor and Divine Healer.

Lord, the psalmist says, "You have searched me and known me...you discern my thoughts from far away...and are acquainted with all my ways" (Ps 139:1–3). Even though you already know all about me, I need to tell you what is bothering me, Lord. My thoughts are racing, confused, angry, and anxious. I need to talk to someone, and you are always available. Please listen, Lord. Correct my wayward thoughts. You are the Truth. Let me think rationally, calmly, without worry.

Banish every thought of self-hatred, despair, or panic which intrudes on my peace.

At times I feel trapped by my fears and anxiety. Release me from these bonds, dear Lord.

You said, "Come apart with me" (see Mt 11:28; Mk 6:31). In prayer I want to distance myself from all that makes me anxious and lay it aside for you to handle. I want to sit at your feet, "to be still and know that you are God" (see Ps 46:10). I want to be confident that you can answer my prayer.

Lord, many things make me angry. This spills into my prayer and spoils my outlook on life. Give me an uplifting life perspective, imbedded in your Gospel teaching. I know that alone I cannot quiet my anger. Direct me to practical means and, if needed, therapy and medicine that can help me manage my emotions. Lord, in the Gospel, a man was gashing himself, and was so tormented that he lived among the tombs (see Mk 5:1–13). At times I feel entombed by this illness. Lay your healing hand on my head. Give me peace, and anchor me in the firm conviction that you love me more than I can ever love myself. Thank you for this love and for listening to me. Amen.

A Prayer to Restore Hope

Have you ever wondered why some people look grim and sad? Often a sad face signifies the absence of a hopeful outlook. With heaven as our goal and God as our anchor, we can always have hope.

Jesus, Risen Lord, companion on the journey to Emmaus (see Lk 24:13–35), my hope in you has sometimes faded. I, too, walked away from Jerusalem and forgot the true joy of your grace. Help me to journey from doubt and fear to recognize you, present in my every step. Teach me to put aside my narrow ideas of who you are. May I never limit your goodness by the confines of my image of who you are.

Help me never to substitute my ego and its wants for you and your will.

May I not insist that you be my very own liberator from earthly troubles, or my private magician who satisfies all my personal wants. I want to recognize you as the Servant who suffered and died so that all may live a new life.

Lead me into your kingdom that is not of this world.

Give me greater faith in your saving death and resurrection.

Grant me a strong hope that sees beyond the confusion and false dreams of this world to your kingdom of love without end. Increase my hope, Lord, so I can accept my own suffering and the suffering of all my brothers and sisters without despair.

Give me more love that pours out the wine of good deeds and gracious words every day. Amen.

Our Shepherd Never Leaves Us

In the Gospel of John, Jesus identifies himself as the Good Shepherd who gives his life for his sheep. Awareness of Christ's love for us leads us to appreciate his care for us. Green pastures may signify peace and calm of soul and the serenity of being secure in the loving arms of Jesus our Good Shepherd.

The LORD is my Shepherd, I shall not want.
    He makes me lie down in green pastures;
he leads me beside still waters;
    he restores my soul.
He leads me in right paths
    for his name's sake.

Even though I walk through the darkest valley,
    I fear no evil;
for you are with me;
    your rod and your staff—
    they comfort me.

You prepare a table before me
    in the presence of my enemies;
you anoint my head with oil;
    my cup overflows.
Surely goodness and mercy shall follow me
    all the days of my life,
and I shall dwell in the house of the LORD
    my whole life long. (Ps 23)

God Wraps Us in His Loving Arms

Has the thought, "No one understands me," ever come into your mind? If it has, this psalm answers the cry of our minds and hearts to be known and understood. The psalmist admits that God certainly knows our thoughts and actions. Before they fly from our lips, God knows our words. We are hemmed in by his goodness and love. If you have ever felt enveloped head-to-foot by the warmth of a comfy blanket on a winter morning, you know the feeling of being hemmed in. God's hem calms and comforts our souls.

O LORD, you have searched me and known me.
You know when I sit down and when I rise up;
   you discern my thoughts from far away.
You search out my path and my lying down,
   and are acquainted with all my ways.
Even before a word is on my tongue,
   O LORD, you know it completely.
You hem me in, behind and before,
   and lay your hand upon me.
Such knowledge is too wonderful for me;
   it is so high that I cannot attain it.

Where can I go from your spirit?
   Or where can I flee from your presence?
If I ascend the heavens you are there;
   if I make my bed in Sheol, you are there.

If I take the wings of the morning
   and settle at the farthest limits of the sea,
even there your hand shall lead me,
   and your right hand shall hold me fast.
If I say, "Surely the darkness shall cover me,
   and the light around me become night,"
even the darkness is not dark to you;
   the night is as bright as the day,
   for darkness is as light to you.

For it was you who formed my inward parts;
   you knit me together in my mother's womb.
I praise you, for I am fearfully and wonderfully made.
   Wonderful are your works;
that I know very well.
   My frame was not hidden from you,
when I was being made in secret,
   intricately woven in the depths of the earth.
Your eyes beheld my unformed substance.
In your book were written
   all the days that were formed for me,
   when none of them as yet existed.
How weighty to me are your thoughts, O God!
   How vast is the sum of them! (Ps 139:1–17)

God, Our Hiding Place

Psalm 32 extols the happiness of one whose sins are forgiven. It also directs us to look to God for safety, for calm, and for peace when we feel overwhelmed by anxiety or our own shortcomings. God indeed is our one truly safe "hiding place."

Therefore let all who are faithful
    offer prayer to you;
at a time of distress, the rush of mighty waters
    shall not reach them.
You are a hiding place for me;
    you preserve me from trouble;
    you surround me with glad cries of deliverance.

I will instruct you and teach you the way you should go;
    I will counsel you with my eye upon you. (Ps 32:6–8)

God Asks Us to Be Still

The Lord asks us to settle down, to relax, and to let him be in charge of our affairs. God, who directs the entire universe, can help us live in true peace of soul.

"Be still, and know that I am God!
    I am exalted among the nations,

I am exalted in the earth."
The LORD of hosts is with us;
>the God of Jacob is our refuge. (Ps 46:10–11)

God Cheers Us

Health issues, financial problems, relational difficulties, and problems of every sort are some of the "wicked rulers" who "band together against the life of the righteous." Psalm 94 points us to God, the source of our lasting joy.

For the LORD will not forsake his people;
>he will not abandon his heritage;
for justice will return to the righteous,
>and all the upright in heart will follow it.

Who rises up for me against the wicked?
>Who stands up for me against evildoers?
If the LORD had not been my help,
>my soul would soon have lived in the land of silence.
When I thought, "My foot is slipping,"
>your steadfast love, O LORD, held me up.
When the cares of my heart are many,
>your consolations cheer my soul.
Can wicked rulers be allied with you,

those who contrive mischief by statute?
They band together against the life of the righteous,
    and condemn the innocent to death.
But the LORD has become my stronghold,
    and my God the rock of my refuge. (Ps 94:14–22)

Have No Fear

God's word offers us a wealth of consolation when stress burdens and discourages us.

One day we will reach God, who sees the whole person we are meant to be. Or, more accurately, God will beckon us to come and be with him forever. Then we will know the truth of the Scriptures that tell us of the good things God has in store for us and the depth of God's love for us.

[D]o not fear, for I am with you,
    do not be afraid, for I am your God;
I will strengthen you, I will help you,
    I will uphold you with my victorious right hand....
For I, the LORD your God,
    hold your right hand;
it is I who say to you, "Do not fear,
    I will help you." (Isa 41:10, 13)

Our Tears Are Precious

Notice the psalmist's honesty: righteously angry, the psalmist asks God to repay his enemies for their misdeeds. As youngsters, we may have been taught to keep quiet in church. Yet the psalms prompt us to be open and frank—even loud—with our God who knows us deeply. The writer admits to shedding tears, confident that these tears are preserved in God's own flask. Our tears are precious to God, who sees when no one else does. As for our enemies, sometimes they are within us: our unruly passions, obsessions, depressions, and addictions.

[M]y enemies trample on me all day long,
  for many fight against me.
O Most High, when I am afraid,
  I put my trust in you.
In God, whose word I praise,
  in God I trust; I am not afraid;
  what can flesh do to me?

All day long they seek to injure my cause;
  all their thoughts are against me for evil.
They stir up strife, they lurk,
  they watch my steps.
As they hoped to have my life,
  so repay them for their crime;
  in wrath cast down the peoples, O God!

You have kept count of my tossings;
    put my tears in your bottle.
    Are they not in your record?
Then my enemies will retreat
    in the day when I call.
    This I know, that God is for me.
In God, whose word I praise,
    in the LORD, whose word I praise,
in God I trust; I am not afraid.
    What can a mere mortal do to me? (Ps 56:2–11)

His Love Endures Forever

*We can extend this psalm's litany of praise by adding our own memories
that confirm our faith in God's enduring and steadfast love.*

O give thanks to the LORD, for he is good,
    for his steadfast love endures forever.
O give thanks to the God of gods,
    for his steadfast love endures forever....
It is he who remembered us in our low estate,
    for his steadfast love endures forever;
and rescued us from our foes,
    for his steadfast love endures forever;

who gives food to all flesh,
for his steadfast love endures forever.

O give thanks to the God of heaven,
for his steadfast love endures forever. (Ps 136:1–2, 23–26)

God Is Near

Psalm 73 speaks directly to God, confident that God, who holds us by the right hand, is the goal of our deepest desires.

...I am continually with you;
you hold my right hand.
You guide me with your counsel,
and afterward you will receive me with honor.
Whom have I in heaven but you?
And there is nothing on earth that I desire other
than you.
My flesh and my heart may fail,
but God is the strength of my heart and my portion
forever. (Ps 73:23–26)

Trust That All Will Be Well

Saint Paul gives us a spiritual "anti-terrorist" weapon to protect us from anxiety.

We know that all things work together for good for those who love God, who are called according to his purpose.... If God is for us, who is against us? He who did not withhold his own Son, but gave him up for all of us, will he not with him also give us everything else? (Rom 8:28, 31–32)

A Promise from God

In this passage from Isaiah we are encouraged by the word to accept God's promise to us. Whenever we read "Israel" or "Jacob" in these Scriptures, we can replace those names with our own to remember that these promises are for all times. God wants to speak to each of us one-on-one.

But now thus says the LORD...
Do not fear, for I have redeemed you;
   I have called you by name, you are mine.
When you pass through the waters, I will be with you;
   and through the rivers, they shall not overwhelm you;
when you walk through fire you shall not be burned,
   and the flame shall not consume you.
For I am the LORD your God,

the Holy One of Israel, your Savior...
Because you are precious in my sight,
    and honored, and I love you.... (Isa 43:1–4)

In the Palm of His Hand

In these words from the prophet Isaiah, each of us is called "Zion." The Lord reminds us today that we are never forsaken.

But Zion said, "The LORD has forsaken me,
    my LORD has forgotten me."
Can a woman forget her nursing child,
    or show no compassion for the child of her womb?
Even these may forget,
    yet I will not forget you.
See, I have inscribed you on the palms of my hands.
(Isa 49:14–16)

Trust in What God Will Do for Us

Pray this Scripture through once. Then read it again replacing your own name for "heavens" and "earth," and then again for "Jerusalem" and "people."

For I am about to create new heavens
    and a new earth;
the former things shall not be remembered
    or come to mind.
But be glad and rejoice forever
    in what I am creating;
for I am about to create Jerusalem as a joy,
    and its people as a delight.
I will rejoice in Jerusalem,
    and delight in my people;
no more shall the sound of weeping be heard in it,
    or the cry of distress....
Before they call I will answer,
    while they are yet speaking, I will hear. (Isa 65:17–19, 24)

When We Feel Powerless

There are times when we feel we have run out of steam and can't go on. In one of the Chronicles of Narnia, *"The Horse and His Boy," the horse assures the boy that he can go on, even though he feels like quitting. Through the consoling words of the prophet Isaiah, God tells us to push on, and he will provide our strength.*

The LORD is the everlasting God,
   the Creator of the ends of the earth.
He does not faint or grow weary;
   his understanding is unsearchable.
He gives power to the faint,
   and strengthens the powerless.
Even youths will faint and be weary,
   and the young will fall exhausted;
but those who wait for the LORD shall renew their strength,
   they shall mount up with wings like eagles,
they shall run and not be weary,
   they shall walk and not faint. (Isa 40:28–31)

Prayers for Special Needs

Comfort for the Grieving

The prophet Isaiah preached to the exiled Jews, devastated at the loss of their temple and land. Many things cause us to mourn, especially the death of a loved one. In this psalm, you may substitute your name for Jerusalem, reflecting that we are members of God's people waiting for salvation.

...He will swallow up death for ever.
Then the Lord GOD will wipe away tears from all faces,
   and the disgrace of his people he will take away from all
     the earth,
   for the LORD has spoken.
It will be said on that day,
   Lo, this is our God; we have waited for him, so that he
     might save us.
   This is the LORD for whom we have waited;
   let us be glad and rejoice in his salvation. (Isa 25:8–9)

Comfort, O comfort my people,
    says your God.
Speak tenderly to Jerusalem,
    and cry to her
that she has served her term,
    that her penalty is paid....
See, the Lord GOD comes with might,
    and his arm rules for him;
his reward is with him,
    and his recompense before him.
He will feed his flock like a shepherd,
    he will gather the lambs in his arms,
and carry them in his bosom,
    and gently lead the mother sheep. (Isa 40:1–2, 10–11)

On the Loss of a Parent

No matter how old we are, the death of a parent leaves a void in our hearts. Only God can give us lasting consolation.

Jesus, console me. You said, "Come to me, all you that are weary and are carrying heavy burdens" (Mt 11:28). My burden of grief is unspeakable, and it feels like others do not understand. You knew what it meant to say goodbye to your foster father,

Saint Joseph. You wept when you lost your friend Lazarus. Thank you for expressing your grief. I am comforted, knowing that you were like us in every way except sin. Lord, help me to live with a new spirit. Allow my loved ones who have passed into eternity to know that I love them dearly. Give me courage and confidence in you to face each new day. I offer you the pain of my grief. May it purify me and make me a gentler, more compassionate person. Turn my sorrow into joy. May I never burden others because of my sense of loss. Give me hope in the eternal reward of heaven where I look forward to seeing my mother and father once again. Amen.

When a Spouse Dies

When a spouse becomes a soul-mate, another self, the couple shares joys and sorrows, hopes and dreams. At death we entrust his or her soul to God's presence in prayer. We are consoled when we think of the thought that "every true act of love lasts for all eternity."

Lord, my beloved has died. Our lives had become one. Our energies and time were spent in building our marriage. Now I feel not only the emptiness of our home, but an emptiness in my heart. I entrust my beloved spouse to your loving arms. If it is your will, let the assurance of his/her presence in your company

comfort me. Give me courage and the will to go on, knowing that your love for me surpasses anything that this world can offer.

Allow me to cherish and enjoy the memories of the happiness we shared and of the sorrows that we embraced together. Give my loved one peace beyond description and eternal happiness. When loneliness overtakes me, remind me that both you and my spouse await me in heaven. Amen.

When an Infant Dies

No human words can express the deep sorrow of the loss of an infant. We commend him or her to the loving arms of God the Father and are consoled knowing that baptism unites us in eternal life.

Jesus, the Gospel says that you invited children to come to you. I know that my little one is already with you, yet this hardly softens my grief. I feel the pain of loss with King David, who wept when his infant son died (cf. 2 Sam 12:15–23). Lord, lift the veil of my grief and give me the grace to accept this loss. I pray that I may live in the light of faith, hope, and love. Grant me confidence in the hope that this little one is an ambassador on behalf of my family with you in heaven. Amen.

For Recovery from Physical Abuse

Physical abuse leaves not only battered and bruised bodies but also deeper soul wounds. Prayer, then, unites us to God's strength and goodness. We ask God to heal all our wounds and to deliver us from all harm.

Lord, through the mystery of your Incarnation, you share in our humanity. I thank you, knowing that my body is your temple. But this temple has been mistreated by those who do not recognize you in me. I feel betrayed and disrespected, unable to trust anyone. Jesus, my Good Shepherd, I want to hide myself in you. By myself I am powerless to forgive those who have wounded me so deeply. You, Divine Physician, can heal where others can only attempt to soothe pain. Lead me to a safe place where I can be in peace. Help me to find healthy ways to express my angry feelings. Protect me from bitterness. I abandon myself totally into your hands. In you and with you I want to forgive those who harmed me. Teach me to love myself because you first loved me. In you I want to become a loving and attentive person. Mary, Mother of Jesus, the Divine Victim, pray for my complete healing. Amen.

For Recovery from Verbal Abuse

At times Jesus healed with just a word. We ask him to heal us of wounds from words that belittled or hurt us in any way.

Lord, I am answering your invitation to "Come to me" (Mt 11:28). I am burdened with years of cutting words, negative remarks, and insulting phrases that wound me deeply. I know that you created me out of love and for love. Yet, I feel so unloved, unappreciated, and scorned. My name and my sense of self-worth have been trampled upon and ground into the dust. Resurrect my self-esteem with the realization that I am truly lovable and that you love me more than I can ever comprehend. Give me the grace to forgive those who have hurt me. Strengthen me to resist the temptation to revenge or bitterness. Teach me the vocabulary of gentleness and affirmation. Transform my hurts into rungs on a ladder that draw me closer to you and render me a more compassionate person. I trust in your goodness and ask deliverance from any further abuse. Amen.

For Healing from Sexual Abuse

Our sexuality is fundamental to our identity. If others misuse this gift and take advantage of us, professional help is usually needed. Even in the aftermath of sexual abuse, one can be comforted in the confidence that God never stops loving us.

Lord, you called me into being and made me good. You graced me with your life in Baptism. Because of this, I can trust that you love me with the tenderness of a mother and the strength of a loving father. Yet things have been done to me that cause me to feel ashamed, unclean, and unworthy. Heal my memory of the wounds of abuse. Restore my self-esteem and heal my fear of intimacy and trust. Help me to build good relationships with others. Keep reminding me that you made all of me good: body and soul. Forgive those who harmed and violated me. Heal them of their disorders. May I never harm others in any way. Grant me courage to begin anew in peace, serenity, confidence, and grace. Amen.

For Healing from Spousal Abuse

The Scriptures depict God as a loving spouse who takes back even the most wayward partner. The wounds and welts inflicted by one who should love us call out for God's loving care.

Jesus, Lord and healer, protect me from harm. The one whom I loved and who promised to love and cherish me has turned against me. The wounds in my soul and psyche are much deeper than the bruises on my body. Heal me, Lord, both inside and out. Give me strength to seek and to persevere in asking for outside help. If my safety and the safety of the rest of my family demand it, give me the fortitude necessary to walk away from this abuse. I commend my spouse to you. I love the person I married, but I fear the person he (or she) has become. I entrust my future to you. You guard my going and my coming. Protect me now and forever. Amen.

To Learn How to Give and Receive Love

The experience of any type of abuse can disrupt one's ability to love and to receive gestures of sincere love. Let us pray for this healing.

Jesus, you are love itself, but I am far from experiencing what love really means. I want to be a truly loving person who both gives and receives love. Teach me to trust and to dismiss my suspicions of others' genuine offers of love and affection. Heal my wounds and guide me so that I may learn how to hold on to love and not let it slip away. Let me accept and cherish acts of love and recognize you reaching out to me through those around me. Mary, mother of the One who is love, teach me to love and be loved. Amen.

To Cope with Job Loss

Losing one's job brings real grief at the loss of income and security. When we are unemployed, we may feel adrift in the dis-ease and humiliation of seeking a new job. God understands and reaches out to us.

Lord, I place all my problems in your hands. I have lost my job. I feel I have lost a major portion of my life. My self-worth is fading. All the security I once enjoyed has disappeared and I have no means of support. Fear of debt and the danger of homelessness are now very real. Lord, your word says that you "hear the cry of the poor." I feel my total poverty at this moment. Give me strength and serenity to face this loss. Teach me to see this as an opportunity to trust in you more deeply. Help me to learn new skills and to be open to the possibility of new directions in my employment that I might receive a sufficient wage for myself and my family. Gift me with great confidence that I will experience a new beginning. I thank you for answering my prayer. Amen.

To Recover from Trauma

The word "trauma" comes from the Greek for wound. Only God can reach down and heal trauma-induced wounds in our psyche. He waits for us to call for help.

Lord, my experience haunts me. Negative events from the past traumatize me and prevent me from growing closer to you. News reports, movies, and events that are insignificant to others trigger memories and feelings that disturb my peace. Lord, I trust my past to your infinite mercy. I know you are with me in the present moment, and I move ahead confident of your providence in the future. Free me from the bonds and the memories that destroy my peace. Heal me with your loving hand. Amen.

To Cope with War-Related Stress

Military combat and its myriad effects can leave us numb and incapable of relating to others. Though seemingly distant, God is closer than we imagine. This prayer helps to unlock our deepest desires for intimacy with the One who never stops loving us.

Lord God, it is hard for me to say formal prayers. I lay open my soul to you and I ask you to heal me. Memories of the past haunt me. At times an unexpected sound provokes me to anger and nervousness. Flashbacks and nightmares trouble my sleep.

Help me to rest peacefully under your watchful gaze. At other times I am unkind to those who love me. I do not mean to hurt them. Help me to ask their pardon and to act in a loving way toward those whom I may have offended. May the trauma I have experienced never cause new suffering for those around me. I feel the burden of my past. Lord, take this load of mental suffering and alleviate my pain. Let me relish the freedom of being loved by you. Amen.

For Comfort After a Natural Disaster

Fires, floods, hurricanes, tornadoes, and storms disrupt our lives and leave us physically and emotionally drained. Media reports of natural disasters can affect emotions so much that we may also feel traumatized. If we should be among those who have suffered loss of family, friends, property, power, food, or water, God is waiting to help us.

Lord, one of your prophets said, "There is devastation on all sides." We too are devastated: homeless, displaced, and now poor in many ways. Thank you for sparing our lives. Give us the courage to clean up without complaints, to find ways of coping, and to help those less fortunate than we are. When our adrenaline fails, give us strength so we can rebuild our lives. Grant us wisdom to do what is best. Give rescue workers and first responders stamina and cheer them on. Prevent us from being over-

come by depression and negativity. Grant wisdom, calm, and energy to our leaders. We trust in you to rebuild our lives. We ask this through your Son Jesus Christ, our Lord. Amen.

For Emotional Recovery from a Natural Disaster

How easily feelings of discouragement and frustration set in after one begins the tiresome work of cleaning up the aftermath of a traumatic event. Here is an honest prayer to help cope with a long-term recovery.

Lord Jesus, you spent thirty years in the house of Nazareth, often doing the same work over and over. You must have felt the monotony and fatigue of sawing logs and shaping hard wood into tools. Have mercy on me. I feel my energy sapped, my patience stretched thin, and I am at my wit's end. All this tedious work is wearing me down. Lord, let me take time to draw a deep breath; to listen to your words: "Do not let your hearts be troubled" (Jn 14:1). Lay your healing hands on my head. Quiet all the thoughts and doubts that race in and out. Drive discouragement and frustration far from me. Give me courage and cheerfulness to complete what I have started without losing patience. Amen.

Prayers for Healing and Deliverance

God Is the Reason for Our Hope

The Book of Lamentations lives up to its title, describing in vivid detail the sufferings of both individuals and the whole nation of biblical Israel. A person today assailed by worry, under stress, and perhaps deprived of family, can relate to this lament. Here the speaker vents despondent feelings to God. Then, like a light turning on, the memory of God's steadfast love takes hold.

[M]y soul is bereft of peace;
  I have forgotten what happiness is;
so I say, "Gone is my glory,
  and all that I had hoped for from the LORD."

The thought of my affliction and my homelessness
  is wormwood and gall!
My soul continually thinks of it
  and is bowed down within me.
But this I call to mind,
  and therefore I have hope:

The steadfast love of the LORD never ceases,
  his mercies never come to an end;
they are new every morning;
  great is your faithfulness. (Lam 3:17–23)

For Those Suffering from Alcohol Addiction

Any addiction holds one prisoner. We ask Jesus, who understands our inner cravings, to free us from the bondage of alcohol addiction.

Jesus, Divine Healer, lay your hands on me and grant me sobriety. I am powerless over alcohol, and my life has become unmanageable. Only you can restore me to sanity. Give me the humility I need to seek help, as well as the fortitude to persevere through my recovery process, especially by reading, attending meetings, and being open with my sponsor, therapist, or spiritual director. Grant my family and friends the gift of support and understanding. With your divine grace, turn my weakness into a new strength of will and a true compassion for my brothers and sisters who share this affliction. Amen.

For Those Suffering from Drug Addiction

Drug dependency spawns a trail of family, social, and health problems. Intimacy with God will free us from the fleeting escape offered by drugs.

Lord, I come to you with complete trust in your power to heal me. My body craves the transitory relief of drugs. Heal the wounds of this addiction and dependency. Give me the will power, the physical stamina, and the courage to detach myself from narcotic fixes. By myself I am powerless, and my life has become unmanageable. I know I need your help and the help of others. Grant me patience with myself and with all my health care providers. In coming clean, I offer you all the discomfort I may endure in reparation for all my excesses. Mary, Help of Christians, pray for me and stay with me as I struggle to gain freedom. Amen.

For Those Who Overeat

Overeating is often symptomatic of a deeper hunger. May our hunger and thirst be for God and the things of God. Then we will nourish ourselves to love and serve God well.

Lord, you alone can satisfy me. Too often I overeat to alleviate my stress and insecurity. Fill the hunger in my heart, which fuels my appetite for food. Replace my weak will with your

strength. Supply me with work and interests that help me to curb my appetite. Grant my family and friends the gift of support and understanding. Let me say "no" to my cravings and "yes" to your grace. Help me to stay away from places and persons who tempt me to overeat. May your fasting for forty days in the desert release me from my disorders. I trust that you will give me this grace. Amen.

For Deliverance from Anorexia or Bulimia

Our culture sends mixed messages: to be attractive, one must be totally thin, and, at the same time, be as strong as an Olympian. The truth lies in treating the body we have with healthful care. Let us ask for the courage to resist the lure of the "perfect body" image, and to serve well the God who loves every ounce of our being!

Jesus, your whole life is an example for us. Many times the Gospel stories find you comfortable at the dinner table. There you nourished your body with food and fed your disciples eternal truths. Teach me to treasure the body you have given me. Allow me to refresh my body by eating enough to sustain myself. Remind me that my life depends on eating adequate meals. When I eat a balanced meal, I am more disposed to pray, work, socialize, and serve you. Free me from an overwhelming desire to diet and to look very thin, or the desire to binge and then purge. Keep me far from those who pressure me and from media or websites that promote an anorexic lifestyle. Thank you for all that you have given me and that you will give me to stabilize my eating and renew my health. Amen.

For Those Suffering from a Gambling Addiction

God is worth far more than any gamble that this world offers! May he free us from the allure of gambling and its effects on family and friends.

Lord, I am helpless without you. In your Gospel you taught us to be good stewards of this world's goods. You said that you came to save what was lost. Gambling causes not only the loss of money, but also, and even more, the loss of self-respect. I turn my will and my life over to your care. With gifts of moderation and self-control, teach me to say "no" when I feel the urge to gamble. Forgive me for the harm I have done to myself, my family, and my friends. Grant me the humility I need to accept help from loved ones, professionals, and support groups. Give me strength to be faithful to my good resolutions. Amen.

To Honor Our Sexuality

Once, while waiting to view a parade from a rooftop garage, I witnessed a scene of temptation and virtue: Three friends strolling down a main street had stopped to inspect the entrance of a bar with "live entertainment." Two went inside while the third refused to go in, remaining on the street. That one said "no" to peer pressure, honored the gift of sexuality, and left an example of Christianity in practice.

Lord, I feel out of control. I feel driven to satisfy my need for intimacy in inappropriate ways. You have made us in your image and likeness. May I respect and honor you, who delight in being with us. Steady my passion and let me use all my energies for your glory. Guide me away from occasions of dangerous curiosity and sin. I ask this through the intercession of Mary, your Mother and mine. Amen.

When Others Speak Ill of Us

Whether delivered in small or large doses, smear campaigns and slander always hurt. We pray God to preserve us from evil words.

Lord, when I hear other people say or do unkind things
    to me,
    help me remember your love for me is all that matters.
Lord, when I feel like people do not appreciate

my work and abilities,
   help me remember your love for me is all that matters.
Lord, when others put me down,
   help me remember your love for me is all that matters.
Lord, when the sky is gray and nothing seems to work
      out well,
   help me remember your love for me is all that matters,
for you are my friend, helper, joy, and happiness!

For Balance

*Both salt and sugar go into a good cake. The right balance makes the differ-
ence: never too much or too little of one ingredient. May God grant us a
sense of calm so we may love without measure and live in serenity and
peace.*

Jesus, Master, you said, "Come after me." Yet, Lord, I feel
myself wandering away from you. I so often feel pulled first in
one direction, then in another. In the rush of frantic activity, I
almost feel outside of my body. Then I come crashing down and
am paralyzed with utter depression. I rarely seem to live happily
on middle ground. Lord, I know that you ride with me on the
seesaw of life. You can do all things. Guide me to achieve balance
in my life. If medication can help me, give me the perseverance
I need to continue a daily regime of medicine. If therapy is good

for me, give me the openness to accept the help of others. Thank you for all the ways you support me. Wrap your strong arms around me and teach me the secrets of your gentle and humble heart. Mary, spouse of the Holy Spirit, work with the Spirit to form Jesus in me. Amen.

To Adjust to a New Environment After a Separation

Children fearful of leaving their mother on the first day of school may tearfully display the pain of their separation anxiety. We may not shed tears or stomp our feet, but we can feel distress when trying to adjust to any new situation.

Jesus, Mary, and Joseph, you knew what it meant to shift from one home to another. You traveled from Bethlehem to Nazareth and to Egypt and back. You were foreigners in a new country. Jesus, you felt the sting of rejection when you returned to your hometown to preach. I need your help to adjust to new surroundings and new people in my life. Remind me that your love surrounded me in the past and will always protect me. Free me from anxiety, nervousness, and undue stress. I trust in your care for me. Dissolve all my fears and grant me serenity. Amen.

A Prayer of Healing and Blessing
for Troubled Hearts

This prayer comes from the heart of Father Gabriele Amorth, who is dedicated to healing ministry for those troubled by demonic influence.[2]

Lord Jesus, you came to heal
our wounded and troubled hearts.
I beg you to heal the torments that
cause anxiety in my heart;
I beg you in a particular way to heal
all who are the cause of sin.
I beg you to come into my life
and heal me of the psychological harms
that struck me in my early years,
and from the injuries that it caused
throughout my life.

Lord Jesus, you know my burdens.
I lay them all on your Good Shepherd's Heart.
I beseech you—by the merits of the great, open
wound in your heart—
to heal the small wounds that are in mine.
Heal the pain of my memories,
so that nothing that has happened to me

will cause me to remain in pain and anguish,
filled with anxiety.

Heal, O Lord,
all those wounds that have been
the cause of all the evil that is rooted in my life.
I want to forgive
all those who have offended me.
Look to those inner sores
that make me unable to forgive.
You who came to forgive the afflicted of heart,
please, heal my own heart.

Heal, my Lord Jesus, those intimate wounds
that cause me physical illness.
I offer you my heart.
Accept it, Lord, purify it, and give me
the sentiments of your Divine Heart....
Make me an authentic witness
to your Resurrection,
your victory over sin and death,
your living presence among us.

For Deliverance from Thoughts of Self-Injury

At times our expectations demand us to be Superman or Superwoman. Then when we fail, we may feel so depressed and angry that we take it out on ourselves physically, causing ourselves harm. Let us pray for God to take control and for the grace to handle the gift of our bodies with great care.

Jesus, Good Shepherd, lay your hand on me. Keep me from inflicting harm on myself. Let me respect my body as your gift, your temple, your property. Let me realize how special and sacred I am. You want to live and work in me. Yet, I feel compelled to hurt myself. As the angel intervened with Abraham, send your angel to stop me from harming myself. Make me aware of your love that surrounds me and seeks my wholeness. Teach me to appreciate all those with whom I live. Heal me from this disorder and give me a peace that rests serenely in you. Amen.

For Deliverance from Self-Harm by Cutting

As a mother soothes her infant, so God wants to console us. Christ knows our sufferings: mental, emotional, moral, or physical, and offers healing. May he teach us to unite our everyday ups and downs with his offering to the Father.

Lord, until now I have sought relief from inner pain, from rage, from my own self-hate, and sometimes from my own numbness by cutting myself. This gives me some release because,

when my pain is on the outside, it's visible. I feel in control. Lord, help me to see *you* as the giver and keeper of my life. Erase the scars on my soul. I have cut my body in hopes of feeling better. It was my attempt to suppress my thoughts of self-hate and anger. You, Divine Healer, can penetrate my inner self and root out the deeper causes of my problems. Heal my heart of all its aching. Teach me how to cope with my anger, my fears, and all my emotions. I know that you love me more than I can ever imagine. Let me accept your love for me and never look for compensation in self-harming behavior. Give me courage and humility so I can seek the professional help I need. Let me accept myself the way you made me and fulfill your dream for me. Deliver me from all thoughts and desires to inflict harm on myself. Lord, I place all my trust in you! Amen.

For Release from Suicidal Thoughts

Extreme depression and even the wrong dosage of a medication can move one to the brink of suicide. Yet every moment of life is a precious gift. Let us pray to cherish and prolong that gift.

Lord, your word commands us to "Choose life!" (Deut 30:19). I feel worthless, trapped in a tunnel of depression. Intrusive and depressing thoughts urge me to do away with life. Yet you tell me, "It is you I want, you I seek." You are the Shepherd risking all to search and find me. Pierce the darkness that chokes and oppresses me. Come to my aid *right now* because nothing seems to encourage me to go on living. I know that you loved me into existence. My faith teaches me that every moment of each life is a gift beyond price. You remind me in Isaiah that *I am precious* (43:4) to you. Lord, save me from destruction. Give me a love for life and the gifts of joy and laughter. Open my eyes to see your love and the love of those who are dear to me. Mary, Queen of all saints, come to help me. Amen.

A Litany for Healing and Release

A friend afflicted with bipolar disease confided that when he is under the cloud of depression, litany-like prayers often help him.

Lord Jesus, you are my Good Shepherd and Healer.
    I come to you, the rock of my salvation, my only
    hope in the darkness of my weakness.

Place your hand on my heart, calm its beating.
    Heal me, Lord Jesus.

Jesus, cast into the sea of your mercy all my negative
    thoughts.
    Jesus, heal my mind.

Jesus, source of peace, you know what disrupts my peace,
    what unnerves and disturbs me and those around me.
    Let the waves of your divine peace wash over me and heal me.

Lord, I cannot concentrate. My fantasy is always in flight.
Hold me still, so I may at least for a moment rest in you and know you better.

Lord, I find myself fidgeting and forgetting about you.
Remind me that you are in charge of my life.

Lord, my horizon is billowing with the darkest of clouds.
Jesus, may your light pierce my darkness.

Lord, I feel so alone. No one seems to truly know what I am going through.
Lord, I trust in you who know me more deeply than any earthly lover can.

Memories of past evils haunt me and tell me I am no good.
Cast painful memories away forever and keep me certain that you made me good and that you love me always.

Lord, I fear crowded places, even churches. Others think me strange and antisocial when I panic.
Console and calm me, Lord. Remind me that you are here protecting me.

Lord, violent thoughts rage through my mind, delusions and negativity swamp me.
Reach down and quiet me. Banish these harmful and chaotic thoughts. Send your Holy Spirit to hold and calm me. Amen.

Postpartum Prayer

After the birth of a child, a mother may experience an unwanted flood of mixed emotions about herself and her baby. God, who became a baby for us, understands the heart of each mother.

Lord, thank you for the blessing of new life in my baby. I know that the miracle of this newborn child is a precious gift of your love, yet my emotions are at their lowest ebb. Right now, I do not feel the joy of a mother and I am ashamed of these feelings. Let me accept this as a passing stage. Supply me with your grace and the medical and emotional treatment that will heal my depression. Help me to be a caring mother. May your Mother inspire me by her example and prayers. Dispel the fog of depression and send me the light of your joy. Amen.

A "Reality Check" Prayer to Overcome Delusions

Saint Augustine wrote, "Lord, that I may know myself, that I may know you!" We ask God for clarity and stability so that, rooted in the assurance of God's love for us, we can blossom into the person God wants us to be.

Lord, deliver me from delusions, vain fantasies, and false thinking. I know that sometimes I perceive persons and things no one else sees; I hear voices no one else hears. When you lived on

this earth, you allowed yourself to be subject to the boundaries and limitations of an ordinary human person. Channel my energies to do my daily tasks well. Keep my imagination in check. Drive far from me anything that is not true and not real. Let me test everything that comes to my mind and only hold to what is good and willed by you. Each day, Lord, grant me the grace to confront my reality with the graces you destined for me. Give me the strength to let go of whatever I alone am hearing and seeing, so that your reality may keep me on a straight path. May I accept your gifts to me and use them for your glory and for the well-being of all my brothers and sisters. Amen.

After an Estrangement

Jesus wept over the death of Lazarus and over the city that rejected him. He knows our feelings and wants to heal the wounds caused by any breakup in our relationships.

Jesus, you are the Light of the World. Right now my world is dark. I am estranged from someone I had loved very much (*here name the person: a relative, a close friend, a co-worker, a neighbor...*). I fear that it was my own fault that this person has left me. Even though I long to restore our friendship, our relationship seems to have dissolved. Lord, I am sorry for anything on my part which drove away my friend. I forgive whatever the other person has done to injure my feelings. Make me a person of compassion. Heal me from this separation anxiety. Grant me a total trust in you. Give me courage to move on and live each day, moment by moment, for you. Mary, Mother of all hope, pray for me. Amen.

For the Obsessive Compulsive Person

Obsessions can exhaust us physically and drain us emotionally, and they may try the patience of those around us. Let us ask God to lead us away from our compulsions and to learn to rest in him.

Lord, the Gospels relate that you released men and women from the bondage of illness. I lay at your feet my neediness that often drives me to excess. These compulsions weary me and sometimes drive a wedge between me and those I love. Admitting my weakness is already a gift from you. Teach me to let go of anything that I don't need; free me from events that are unnecessary; keep me away from habits that destroy my peace and damage my relationships. Keep me from projecting my obsessions on others. Liberate me from perfectionism and the urge to do everything. Penetrate my layers of need. Let me "be still and know that you are God" (see Ps 46:10). You are in charge; I don't need to be in control of everything. Lay your healing hands on me to free me from the bonds of my obsessions. Give me the peace that only you can give. Amen.

To Cope with Bipolar Disorder

If you have ever seen Maine's rocky shoreline, you have watched tides crashing in and spilling over seawalls. Then the water rushes back to the center of the sea. Yet there are rocks high enough to remain above the changing tides. God is the Rock who steadies us no matter which pole is pulling.

Lord, one of the psalms tells us that you are our "rock of refuge" (cf. Ps 18). Center my life in you so that I may have a holy balance of prayer, work, service, and relaxation. My sickness pulls me in opposite directions. I can swing from frenzied activity to deep depression. Keep me faithful to my daily medications, my therapies, and my spiritual director so I may grow closer to you every day. Heal my broken relationships and grant me your peace. Amen.

Judith's Prayer for Deliverance

Holofernes and his army intimidated all the male leaders of the Israelite city. Judith turned to God for help with fasting and earnest prayer while she disciplined herself in penitential garb. Her prayer was heard. Her beauty charmed the enemy general and she then was able to destroy him. Like Judith, we can turn from distractions, fast from a favorite food, a TV show, or an Internet site, and focus instead on our present need as we pray with Judith's words.

"Please, please, God of my father, God of the heritage of Israel, Lord of heaven and earth, Creator of the waters, King of all your creation, hear my prayer!... Let your whole nation and every tribe know and understand that you are God, the God of all power and might, and that there is no other who protects the people of Israel but you alone!" (Jdt 9:12, 14)

Esther's Prayer for Deliverance

Our enemies—an addiction, an illness, or a relational difficulty—can oppress us. Like Mordecai and his niece, Queen Esther, devout Jews in exile, we can ask God to turn our sorrow into joy!

"And now, O Lord God and King, God of Abraham, spare your people; for the eyes of our foes are upon us to annihilate us, and they desire to destroy the inheritance that has been yours from the beginning. Do not neglect your portion, which you redeemed for yourself out of the land of Egypt. Hear my prayer; have mercy upon your inheritance; turn our mourning into feasting....

"O my Lord, you only are our king; help me, who am alone and have no helper but you.... But save us by your hand, and help me, who am alone and have no helper but you, O Lord." (Esth C13:15–17, C14:3, 14)

A Prayer for Deliverance from the Evil One

The author of this prayer is engaged full time in the ministry of deliverance of the extremely troubled from the shackles of demonic attacks.[3]

My Lord, you are all powerful, you are God, you are Father. We beg you through the intercession and help of the archangels Michael, Raphael, and Gabriel for the deliverance of our brothers and sisters who are enslaved by the evil one. All saints of heaven come to our aid.

From anxiety, sadness, and obsessions.
We beg you. Free us, O Lord.

From hatred, fornication, envy.
We beg you. Free us, O Lord.

From thoughts of jealousy, rage, and death.
We beg you. Free us, O Lord.

From every thought of suicide.
We beg you. Free us, O Lord.

From every form of sinful sexuality.
We beg you. Free us, O Lord.

From every division in our family and every harmful friendship.
We beg you. Free us, O Lord.

From every sort of spell, malefice, witchcraft, and every form
of the occult.
We beg you. Free us, O Lord.

Lord, you who said, "I leave you peace, my peace I give you,"
grant that, through the intercession of the Virgin Mary, we may
be liberated from every evil spell and enjoy your peace always. In
the name of Christ, our Lord. Amen.

A Prayer for Help

*In this Bible prayer, the writer praises God and asks for seven favors. The
mood ranges from the heights of heaven in praising God to the pit of Sheol.
But the praise that is God's gift to us as much as our gift back to God,
supernatural joy, is not always felt. It is higher than emotion. Ancients
considered the after world—or Sheol—to be dark, buried in the depths of
the earth. Our troubles may make us feel as if we have been cast into
Sheol. Here we trust that God will give us an undivided heart so we can
continue to praise him with our lives and words.*

Incline your hear, O LORD, and answer me,
for I am poor and needy.
Preserve my life, for I am devoted to you;
save your servant who trusts in you.
You are my God; be gracious to me, O LORD,
for to you do I cry all day long.

Gladden the soul of your servant,
  for to you, O LORD, I lift up my soul.
For you, O LORD, are good and forgiving,
  abounding in steadfast love to all who call on you.
Give ear, O LORD, to my prayer;
  listen to my cry of supplication.
In the day of my trouble I call on you,
  for you will answer me. (Ps 86:1–7)

To Overcome Sadness

Even on a sunny day we might feel blue or melancholy for no apparent reason. At these times we ask God to allow the warmth and light of Jesus' goodness to penetrate the darkness of our souls.

Lord, you promised us joy that "no one can take away." I feel locked in a chamber of sad thoughts that no ray of light seems to penetrate. Dissolve the bonds of my sadness, and let me smile once again. Your servant, Sister Thecla Merlo of the Daughters of Saint Paul, once wrote, "Even if we cannot always be joyful, we can always be at peace." Grant me your peace, Lord, which penetrates the recesses of my soul and gives me the unbounded joy of a beloved child of God. I ask this through Jesus, the healing Sun of justice. Amen.

A Sacramental Touch

THE SACRAMENTS ARE often described as "outward signs of inward grace." Like a kiss between lovers, the sacraments both symbolize and truly bring about that beautiful intimacy that we call grace. We touch or taste things like bread, wine, water, or oil, and we hear the words of blessing. We encounter God's healing touch.

A Prayer Before the Celebration of the Eucharist

In the celebration of the Eucharist we can immerse our time-bound and often troubled lives into Christ's paschal mystery of dying and rising. The Mass does not remove the causes of our anxiety, but it provides us with grace to face them with courage from on high.

Jesus, Risen Lord, abide with us. Bring us to your table. Many of your people suffer poverty, hunger, oppression, and death. Bring us to the table with the neighbor and the stranger. Forgive me all my failings and sins. Let me share my talents and gifts with those who are near to me—family, coworkers and neighbors. I believe that you are truly present in the word, in all of us gathered in the assembly, in the priest, in the Sacred Host, and in the Precious Blood. I adore you present in the sacrament of the Holy Eucharist. May I welcome you with all my heart and soul. Stay with me and make me your ambassador of goodness and love. Thank you for this privilege. May I always be aware of your presence in the sacramental breaking of the Bread. Amen.

A Prayer Before the Sacrament of Reconciliation

If we ever think that God has abandoned us—because of our own failures or misfortunes—it helps to remember that God loves us, no matter what situation we are in. In the Sacrament of Reconciliation, God awaits us to console us and to assure us of the forgiveness of our sins and failings.

Lord, I thank you for being available and ready to listen to me in the person of your priest. Send your Holy Spirit to enlighten me so I may know my sins and confess them clearly. I am truly sorry for every offense I may have committed against you, my God, and against any other person. I resolve sincerely and firmly, with your grace, to sin no more and to avoid the occasions of sin. Protect me from scruples and anxiety. May I listen attentively to the confessor's advice and the words of absolution. I lay my sins at your feet and know that you will cast them into the sea of your divine mercy. Amen.

God Forgives

Some people say, "How can God forgive me?" when their sins and faults seem too vile and offensive to present to God. Our Father knows our inner-most needs and is eager to heal and love us freely.

I will heal their disloyalty;
   I will love them freely,
     for my anger has turned from them....
     It is I who answer and look after you. (Hos 14:4, 8)

Come now...says the LORD:
though your sins are like scarlet,
   they shall be like snow;
though they are red like crimson,
   they shall become like wool. (Isa 1:18)

To Have a Contrite Heart

Habits of sin, clinging to grudges, wasting time in the cellar of self-pity and useless fantasies can really trouble one's heart. Psalm 25 pleads to God about our foes and troubles.

Turn to me and be gracious to me,
   for I am lonely and afflicted.

Relieve the troubles of my heart,
    and bring me out of my distress.
Consider my affliction and my trouble,
    and forgive all my sins.

Consider how many are my foes,
    and with what violent hatred they hate me.
O guard my life, and deliver me;
    do not let me be put to shame, for I take refuge in you.
May integrity and uprightness preserve me,
    for I wait for you. (Ps 25:16–21)

David's Contrition

Israel's King David, the shepherd boy and giant slayer, is a perennial Bible hero. Beloved as he was, David sinned by committing adultery and then murder to cover up his sin. Psalm 51, often called by its Latin title, the Miserere, expresses David's sincere repentance and sorrow:

Indeed, I was born guilty,
    a sinner when my mother conceived me.

You desire truth in the inward being;
    therefore teach me wisdom in my secret heart.
Purge me with hyssop, and I shall be clean;

wash me, and I shall be whiter than snow.
Let me hear joy and gladness;

    let the bones that you have crushed rejoice.
Hide your face from my sins,

    and blot out all my iniquities.

Create in me a clean heart, O God,

    and put a new and right spirit within me....
The sacrifice acceptable to God is a broken spirit;

    a broken and contrite heart, O God, you will not despise.
(Ps 51:5–10, 17)

Following Jesus and Pondering
with Mary, His Mother

TWO FAVORITE CATHOLIC devotions are the Way of the Cross
and the Rosary of our Lady. May these reflections help those
who feel oppressed by anxiety, stress, or other troubles to lay
down their burdens and to rest their souls in the presence of Jesus
and his Mother Mary.

A Way of the Cross
for Moments of Vulnerability

*The Way of the Cross, also called the Stations, helps Christians retrace the
journey Jesus made to Calvary. When possible, pray these in a church or
shrine where the images of the Way are displayed. If this is not convenient,
you can pray the Stations anywhere. Traditionally we begin each station by
praying: "We adore you, O Christ, and we bless you, because by your holy
cross you have redeemed the world."*

✠ THE FIRST STATION ✠
The Condemnation

Pilate...took some water and washed his hands before the crowd, saying: "I am innocent of this man's blood; see to it yourselves" (Mt 27:24).

You died for me, Lord Jesus. You accepted your sentence without a murmur—only love. With you, Lord, I too say, "Not my will, but yours be done, O Father."

✠ THE SECOND STATION ✠
Jesus Accepts His Cross

[A]nd carrying the cross by himself, [Jesus] went out.... "If any want to become my followers, let them deny themselves and take up their cross and follow me" (Jn 19:17; Mt 16:24).

Jesus, you accepted the cross for me. Experts tell us that the cross beam was laid on your shoulders and was fastened to your arms by ropes. You must have doubled over in pain as its unrelenting pressure reopened your wounds. How often old wounds from my past are reopened by a painful memory, a song, a scent, a glance....

You said, "I have eagerly desired to eat this Passover with you" (Lk 22:15). You accepted utter powerlessness for me and wanted to show your love and patience by accepting this cross. My cross can be so heavy: medications without end, moods that come and go like the wind, loss of friends, setbacks at work, my failures, and grief of all kinds. You embraced your cross and showed me how to carry mine day by day, minute by minute. As you shouldered that burden, you saw me and you loved me. Thank you for going before me to be my Way.

✠ THE THIRD STATION ✠
Jesus Falls Beneath the Cross

He was despised and rejected…we held him of no account.
Surely he has borne our infirmities and carried our diseases….
(Isa 53:3–4).

Jesus, you trip and fall, striking your head on the pavement. You cannot shield yourself. Your face was already bruised; now it is scraped and marred. You fell, and yet you struggled to your feet for me. It wasn't easy. Some in the crowd mocked you. Others cursed you as a criminal. By accepting these cruel remarks, Lord, you help me endure the remarks others make about me. At times moods, fits of anger, or dense clouds of depression strike me down. Everything seems so chaotic. Some people pitied you as they remembered your smile and healing words. By your fall, heal me, Lord. Cool my temper, calm my nerves, soothe my anxiety. By myself, I know I am incapable of rising from these falls. With you, Lord, I can get up and move on.

✠ THE FOURTH STATION ✠
Jesus Meets His Mother

Simeon...said to his mother Mary, "...and a sword will pierce your own soul too" (Lk 2:35).

Jesus, your eyes—swollen and smarting with dirt, spittle, and blood—meet those of your mother. This moment is meant to be a gesture of solace and love. It hurts you deeply to see your mother's pain as she looks on you, the light of her eyes. You long to spare her this humiliation. You long to shield her ears from the whispers and shouts: "Look, there is the mother of that impostor, that criminal, that blasphemer!" Your mother does not shrink from your pain. She stands by you. In accepting each other's pain, you—Son and mother—somehow console one another. Mary brought you into the world; she will be with you as you leave it. I pray now for mothers and fathers of those who suffer from mental distress. May they see you, Lord, in their children who seem so distant, disturbed, and sad. As your glance must have strengthened your mother's heart, give courage and consolation to the parents and families of those who carry the cross of mental illness or anxiety.

Simon of Cyrene Lifts the Weight of the Cross

As they went out, they came upon a man from Cyrene named Simon; they compelled this man to carry his cross (Mt 27:32).

Jesus, the soldiers realized that you would collapse before reaching Calvary. They forced Simon to carry your cross for you. You accepted that help. What a wonder: God the Almighty accepting help from a laboring man. Lord, help me accept the offers of Cyrenians who come into my life. Help me to cast off my cloak of denial and say *yes* and *thank you* to those who care enough to offer to alleviate some of my pain and loneliness. When it's my turn to be a Simon of Cyrene, let me remember that others are in pain—not just me. Give me the spiritual insight to know the invitations you send me to lift the burden from another's shoulders—if only with a smile, a listening ear, or the promise of a prayer.

✠ The Sixth Station ✠
Veronica Wipes the Face of Jesus

Look on my misery and rescue me,
for I do not forget your law (Ps 119:153).

Jesus, Veronica cared enough to approach you and press her veil to your holy face. You repaid her kindness by leaving your image on that makeshift towel. In the Garden of Gethsemane, you suffered an agony of fear, dread, and loneliness. Let me see you in those faces lined with the terror of panic attacks, marks of anxiety, trauma, fear, desolation, and distrust. Jesus, imprint your image firmly in my soul, that others may see you in my actions, recognize you in my gaze, and hear your voice in mine.

✠ The Seventh Station ✠
Jesus Falls a Second Time

But I am a worm, and not human;
scorned by others, and despised by the people (Ps 22:6).

Lord, tradition tells us that you fell at least three times under the cross. Your weakened condition must have caused you to stumble over and over. Each time the fatigue was more and more oppressive, the pain more searing. How often I am tired of being sick, of being labeled less fit than others. I tire of physicians, psychiatrists, counselors, prescriptions, and advice. Worse yet, Lord, I fear a relapse, another fall into deep wells of addiction, depression, or storms of uncontrollable anger. As you forced yourself to rise from the pavement, you strengthen me to rise from my lapses, my depressions and bad days. Thank you, Lord, for getting up and moving on for me.

✠ THE EIGHTH STATION ✠
Jesus Meets the Women of Jerusalem

Jesus turned to them and said, "Daughters of Jerusalem, do not weep for me, but weep for yourselves and for your children" (Lk 23:28).

At last, Jesus, you meet some people who feel compassion for you, the women who were crying and beating their breasts in sorrow at your agony. You were wracked with thirst. Your mouth had been slapped so many times that your lips were swollen and cracked. Yet you made the effort to acknowledge their pity and spoke of the need for repentance from all sin. I find certain observations about me hard to accept. Let me see you, Lord, in those who try to help me, and even in those who contradict or criticize me. Thank you for teaching me with your example, even as you walked to Calvary.

✠ THE NINTH STATION ✠
Jesus Falls a Third Time Beneath the Cross

But he was wounded for our transgressions,
crushed for our iniquities;
upon him was the punishment that made us whole
and by his bruises we are healed (Isa 53:5).

Once again you are pinned beneath the weight of the cross. Everything in you clamored to give up, to die in the streets of Jerusalem. Yet you were resolved to reach Calvary. You said, "And I, when I am lifted up from the earth, will draw all people to myself" (Jn 12:32). On Calvary you would be lifted high so all could see how much you loved us. Only a supreme effort of your love for me brought you back on your feet to continue your journey. When grief or depression seems to strangle me, keeps me from interacting with others, or prevents me from seeing any good, let me think of you, Lord, and your call to get up, take up my cross, and continue to follow in your footsteps today.

✠ THE TENTH STATION ✠
Jesus Is Stripped of His Garments

[T]hey cast lots to divide his clothing (Lk 23:34).

Now, Jesus, you are stripped to heal our humanity. You are deprived of clothing, prestige, identity. You are naked to clothe me with divine life. How often illness like mine robs me of my identity. I feel disassociated at times, distanced from others and even myself; I hardly know myself. There are times when I may even be deluded and agitated. I can't seem to settle down, to find peace with myself. By the mystery of your passion, Lord, clothe me with wholeness of mind and body.

✠ THE ELEVENTH STATION ✠
Jesus Is Nailed to the Cross

[T]hey crucified Jesus there with the criminals, one on his right and one on his left. Then Jesus said, "Father, forgive them; for they do not know what they are doing" (Lk 23:33–34).

Lord, as though you were the worst of criminals, you are crucified in the company of thieves. Three enormous spikes fastened your sacred body to the wood. Those nails denied you freedom of movement. Every breath was a torture. With those

nails, Saint Paul said, you "nailed our sins to the cross" (see Col 2:13–15). Yet you gave your life freely for me. You forgave the thief dying next to you and those who caused your death. You forgive me now. Lord, I believe that every Eucharistic Celebration renews the power of your sacrifice. Even when I am in the darkest night, let me come to you in the Mass and unite my crucifixion to yours. Help me also to forgive those who have hurt me, those who misunderstand or fail to accept me.

✠ THE TWELFTH STATION ✠
Jesus Dies on the Cross

[Jesus] said (in order to fulfill the scripture), "I am thirsty." A jar full of sour wine was standing there. So they put a sponge full of the wine on a branch of hyssop and held it to his mouth. When Jesus had received the wine, he said, "It is finished." Then he bowed his head and gave up his spirit.... [O]ne of the soldiers pierced his side with a spear, and at once blood and water came out (Jn 19:28–30, 34).

Jesus, you suffered tremendous thirst throughout your passion. Even in the Garden of Gethsemane when you sweat blood, you must have craved a soothing drop of cold water. Yet we know from spiritual masters that your greatest thirst is your love for us. You thirst for men and women to come to you, to come to your pierced heart, to quench our thirst for genuine love. When I thirst for comfort, strength, and love, let me not seek relief in addiction or unhealthy means, but in you, Jesus. You died for me; let me live the gift of life in its fullness for you.

✠ THE THIRTEENTH STATION ✠
Jesus Is Taken Down from the Cross

[A] good and righteous man named Joseph...went to Pilate and asked for the body of Jesus (Lk 23:50, 52).

Joseph of Arimathea and his friend Nicodemus were members of the Sanhedrin that condemned you, Jesus. These two men, concerned for you, ignored the possible consequences of their actions and approached Pilate to ask for your body. Pilate granted their request and they, along with the women followers, prepared your body for burial. Tradition says that the two friends laid your body in Mary's lap. The wounds left by the indignities and tortures you suffered for each of us pierced her heart. Let me remain with Mary to console her in her grief. My silent presence is a sign of my love. As Nicodemus and Joseph consoled Mary, may I be present to others in their pain and grief, especially those who are misunderstood or rejected and living under the stigma of mental illness or addiction.

✠ FOURTEENTH STATION ✠
Jesus' Body Is Laid in the Tomb

So Joseph [of Arimathea] took the body and wrapped it in a clean linen cloth and laid it in his own new tomb, which he had hewn in the rock. He then rolled a great stone to the door of the tomb and went away (Mt 27:59–60).

Jesus, you suffered a real death. Your body was laid to rest, away from the normal bustle of daily life, in the quiet of the tomb. Some day this will happen to me, too.

The Creed tells us that you "descended to the dead," or to the hell, the *Sheol,* of the ancients. Sometimes life with mental illness or other disorders seems like a burial, cut off from the land of the living, and a shunting to a sort of death. As you accepted your burial, Lord, I accept the daily dyings presented to me. I only ask for the grace to follow you, step by step, knowing that the resurrection will come as surely as the dawn.

The Resurrection of Jesus

[T]he angel said to the women, "Do not be afraid; I know that you are looking for Jesus who was crucified. He is not here; for he has been raised, as he said. Come, see the place where he lay" (Mt 28:5–6).

Your resurrection is the keystone of my faith. Saint Augustine said, "We are Easter people, and *alleluia* is our song." There are times when things seem so terrifying, and my mood is so dark, that I must confess: I tire of rejoicing. Sometimes I find the somberness of Lent easier to take than all the joy that the *alleluias* force on me. Give me joy, Lord, and lift me from worry, anxiety, and the paralysis of depression. Make me a real *alleluia* person. Lord, you are my hope. Let me never be disappointed.

The Mysteries of the Rosary

A homilist once said that carrying a rosary is like carrying the Gospel in your pocket. The two main prayers of the Rosary, the Our Father and the Hail Mary, are taken from the Gospel and offer meditations on the life of Jesus and Mary. (See the origins of the Hail Mary in Lk 1:28, 31, 42; and the Our Father, the Lord's Prayer, in Mt 6:9–13 and Lk 11:2–4.) That is why the Rosary can be called a portable or pocket Gospel.

To pray the Rosary, we engage in two kinds of prayer: mental prayer—because we think about the life of Jesus and Mary, and of our own—and vocal prayer. We may say the prayers aloud, whisper the prayers, or move our lips silently if we are in a place with others around us. Some rosary beads are shaped like rose buds, since the prayers are meant to form a spiritual bouquet of roses offered to Jesus through Mary.

To pray the Rosary with rosary beads, begin like this: On the crucifix, pray the Apostles' Creed. On the next bead, pray the Our Father (the Lord's Prayer). On each of the three beads that follow, pray a Hail Mary to ask for the virtues of faith, hope, and Christian charity. Then pray a "Glory be to the Father...."

On the connecting bead or medallion, begin the mysteries: quietly reflect on the life of Jesus and Mary. Announce the mystery: for example, "The first Joyful Mystery: the Annunciation." Then pray the Lord's Prayer. On the ten beads that follow, pray a Hail Mary for each bead. On the chain or cord that separates the decade (the set of ten beads), pray: "Glory be to the Father, and to the Son, and to the Holy Spirit: as it was in the beginning, is now, and will be for ever. Amen." While our lips are praying the Hail Marys, our minds are thinking about what the mystery signifies. After the Glory Be, announce the second mystery and then pray the Our Father, ten Hail Marys, and the Glory Be. This process is repeated for each mystery.

Here follows a Scripture reading for every mystery, and a meditative prayer to apply the lesson of the event to our lives. At times just a word or a phrase may be enough for reflection throughout the mystery.

We divide the mysteries into four sets of five episodes in the life of Jesus and Mary. The four kinds of mysteries are the Joyful, the Luminous, the Sorrowful, and the Glorious. Some people are able to pray all twenty mysteries every day. For others, the effort to pray a decade is a prayer well done.

The Lord's Prayer

Our Father, who art in heaven, hallowed be thy name;
thy kingdom come;
thy will be done on earth as it is in heaven.
Give us this day our daily bread,
and forgive us our trespasses,
as we forgive those who trespass against us.

And lead us not into temptation;
but deliver us from evil. Amen.

Hail Mary

Hail Mary, full of grace,
the Lord is with you.
Blessed are you among women
and blessed is the fruit of your womb, Jesus.
Holy Mary, Mother of God, pray for us sinners,
now and at the hour of our death. Amen.

Apostles' Creed

I believe in God, the Father almighty,
creator of heaven and earth.
I believe in Jesus Christ, his only Son, our Lord.
He was conceived by the power of the Holy Spirit and
born of the Virgin Mary.
He suffered under Pontius Pilate, was crucified, died, and
was buried.
He descended to the dead.
On the third day he rose again.
He ascended into heaven, and is seated at the right hand
of the Father.

He will come again to judge the living and the dead.
I believe in the Holy Spirit,
the holy catholic Church,
the communion of saints,
the forgiveness of sins,
the resurrection of the body,
and the life everlasting. Amen.

Glory to the Father

Glory to the Father, and to the Son, and to the Holy Spirit: as it was in the beginning, is now, and will be for ever. Amen.

Hail Holy Queen

Hail, holy Queen, Mother of mercy,
hail, our life, our sweetness, and our hope.
To you we cry, the children of Eve;
to you we send up our sighs,
mourning, and weeping in this land of exile.
Turn, then, most gracious advocate,
your eyes of mercy toward us;
lead us home at last
and show us the blessed fruit of your womb, Jesus:
O clement, O loving, O sweet Virgin Mary.

The Joyful Mysteries
The Mysteries of the Hidden Life

The Joyful Mysteries of the Rosary center on the lives of Jesus, Mary, and Joseph, especially as they carried out the will of God in Nazareth. Blessed James Alberione called the thirty-year period of Jesus' hidden life the "School of Nazareth." In silence and hiddenness, Jesus, the Master Teacher, began to teach us his lessons of obedience to his parents, attention to his duties as a carpenter, and all the virtues, particularly lived out in a family.

THE FIRST JOYFUL MYSTERY

The Annunciation

In the sixth month the angel Gabriel was sent by God to a town in Galilee called Nazareth, to a virgin engaged to a man whose name was Joseph, of the house of David. The virgin's name was Mary. And he came to her and said, "Greetings, favored one! The Lord is with you." But she was much perplexed by his words and pondered what sort of greeting this might be. The angel said to her, "Do not be afraid, Mary, for you have found favor with God. And now, you will conceive in your womb and bear a son, and you will name him Jesus...." Then Mary said, "Here am I, the servant of the Lord; let it be with me according to your word" (Lk 1:26–31, 38).

The Archangel Gabriel announces to Mary the good news that she will be mother of the Messiah, that is, Mother of God. Mary's *yes* held consequences for her. Some would sneer at her unexpected pregnancy and doubt her integrity. Yet she accepted Gabriel's invitation because she trusted in the God who loved her. Her *yes* led to eternal joy for her and for us. Let us ask the grace to imitate Mary's trust, especially when we feel shunned or mistrusted.

THE SECOND JOYFUL MYSTERY

The Visit to St. Elizabeth

In those days Mary set out and went with haste to a Judean town in the hill country, where she entered the house of Zechariah and greeted Elizabeth. When Elizabeth heard Mary's greeting, the child leaped in her womb (Lk 1:39–41).

Often our personality difficulties turn us inward, blocking out the needs of those around us. Mary did not hesitate to go out of her way and to lend a hand as soon as she realized her elderly cousin's need. Her visit brought joy to Elizabeth and Zechariah and to the yet-to-be-born John the Baptist. Let us ask the grace to help family members, coworkers, caregivers, and all who cross our path. Our help may be just a smile or a word of thanks. Yet, like Mary, we can bring Jesus and his joy to others as she did.

The Birth of Jesus in the Stable of Bethlehem

And she gave birth to her firstborn son and wrapped him in bands of cloth, and laid him in a manger, because there was no place for them in the inn (Lk 2:7).

Mary carried within her the Light of the World. Through the centuries people have cried out, "Joy to the world!" Yet Mary and Joseph met rejection, because "there was no room where travelers lodged." Perhaps it was their poverty that made others close their doors. From the moment of his birth, our Savior felt the deprivation of poverty. He also felt the love and affection given by the poorest—the shepherds, Mary and Joseph. Illness— both emotional and physical—is a form of poverty. Let us ask the grace to unite the poverty of our disorders with Jesus, who was pleased to be laid in a manger for us. Let us ask, too, for release from the pressure of grasping for the passing riches of this world.

THE FOURTH JOYFUL MYSTERY

The Presentation of the Child Jesus in the Temple

When the time came for their purification according to the law of Moses, they brought him up to Jerusalem to present him to the Lord.... Then Simeon blessed them and said to his mother Mary, "This child is destined for the falling and the rising of many in Israel, and to be a sign that will be opposed so that the inner thoughts of many will be revealed—and a sword will pierce your own soul too." …[Anna] came, and began to praise God and to speak about the child to all who were looking for the redemption of Jerusalem (Lk 2:22, 34–35,38).

The elderly Simeon and Anna both recognized the One who was resting in Mary's arms. Mary pondered Simeon's words in her heart. One day the sword of sorrow that Simeon foresaw would strike deep into Mary's heart. When sorrow pierces our hearts, too, let us ask Mary for the grace to discern God's presence, even amidst the chaos and pain.

THE FIFTH JOYFUL MYSTERY

The Losing and Finding of Jesus

[W]hen he was twelve years old, they went up as usual for the festival. When the festival was ended and they started to return, the boy Jesus stayed behind in Jerusalem, but his parents did not know it…. When they did not find him, they returned to Jerusalem to search for him. After three days they found him in the temple, sitting among the teachers, listening to them and asking them questions (Lk 2:42–43, 45–46).

This is a moment when Mary and Joseph certainly experienced their "dark night," perhaps their first one after the sojourn in Egypt. What was it like to be without their Son, God's Beloved? They must have felt on the edge of despair, assailed by

fear, panic, and a numbing sense of loss. We can contemplate how the dark night of this holy couple was dispelled by finding their Son, the Lord, safe and "about his father's business." In this mystery, we ask the grace to do God's will despite clouds of depression, sadness, and spiritual aridity. We will then find Jesus in the temple of our hearts.

The Mysteries of Light
Events of Jesus' Public Ministry

In the Mysteries of Light we contemplate Jesus, who brought light to the world through his examples, preaching, and miracles.

THE FIRST MYSTERY OF LIGHT
The Baptism of Jesus in the Jordan

> *Now when all the people were baptized, and when Jesus also had been baptized and was praying, the heaven was opened, and the Holy Spirit descended upon him in bodily form like a dove. And a voice came from heaven, "You are my Son, the Beloved; with you I am well pleased" (Lk 3:21–22).*

After Jesus spent time in the desert in fasting and prayer, he came to the banks of the Jordan River where John the Baptist was immersing people in a baptism of repentance. At first John did not recognize Jesus standing in line with those awaiting baptism. Although he was sinless, Jesus allowed himself to be identified with the sinners in need of repentance. Once he recognized Jesus, John tried to stop him. "You should baptize me," he insisted. Jesus prevailed and was baptized. When John gave in, all heaven broke open. The Holy Spirit came and God the Father spoke: "This is my beloved Son!" Jesus' submission to baptism opened the heavens. I ask the grace to submit to treatments, medications, and even long-term care for the love of him who "became like us in all things except sin."

The Wedding Feast of Cana

> *When the wine gave out, the mother of Jesus said to him, "They have no wine." And Jesus said to her, "Woman, what concern is that to you and to me? My hour has not yet come." His mother said to the servants, "Do whatever he tells you" (Jn 2:3–5).*

We see Jesus and his disciples joining the guests to share in the joy of a wedding feast. Mary, his mother, realizes that something has gone amiss. The wine is running out. With her maternal thoughtfulness, Mary knows that her Son can save the day for the newlyweds. At the urging of his mother, who told the waiters to "do whatever he tells you," Jesus transforms water into wine. John's Gospel calls this miraculous transformation at Cana the "first of [Jesus'] signs" (Jn 2:11).

May Jesus work his signs in us and change the water of our deeds into the wine of love for God and our neighbor. We pray also for married couples, that the wine of their mutual love may grow more precious with each passing year. We pray especially for those in troubled or abusive marriages, the separated and divorced, as well as couples living together without the sacrament of Matrimony.

THE THIRD MYSTERY OF LIGHT

Jesus Begins the Preaching of the Gospel

Jesus went throughout Galilee, teaching in their synagogues and proclaiming the good news of the kingdom and curing every disease and every sickness among the people (Mt 4:23).

In this mystery, we ponder the powerful gift of the Gospel that Jesus began to preach. The Gospel reveals the Good News that God, through Jesus, has stepped into time to be one of us, to redeem us, and to bring us safely home. "Repent and believe the Good News" was his message. Saint Paul said he was "not ashamed of the Gospel" (Rom 1:16). It's often said that the only Gospel some people may read will be our lives. Let us ask the grace to be "living Gospels," and let us trust that the Gospel message will bring us light in the midst of darkness and courage in the midst of trials.

THE FOURTH MYSTERY OF LIGHT

The Transfiguration of Jesus

And while he was praying, the appearance of his face changed, and his clothes became dazzling white.... [A] cloud came and over-shadowed them...from the cloud came a voice that said, "This is my Son, my Chosen; listen to him!" (Lk 9:29, 34–35)

In this mystery, Jesus allows the apostles a glimpse of his divinity. The Transfiguration reminds us of the glory and freedom of heaven. Jesus' clothes were shining and Moses and Elijah were with him. Jesus was speaking to them about his passion. When intrusive thoughts darken our horizons or suspicion sullies our relationships, let us ask the glorified and transfigured Lord Jesus to heal us.

THE FIFTH MYSTERY OF LIGHT

Jesus Gives the Gift of His Body and Blood in the Eucharist

He took a loaf of bread, and when he had given thanks, he broke it and gave it to them, saying, "This is my body, which is given for you. Do this in remembrance of me." And he did the same with the cup after supper, saying, "This cup that is poured out for you is the new covenant in my blood" (Lk 22:19–20).

Jesus promised to be with us until the end of time. In the liturgy of the Eucharist he allows us to remember his love for us

and to be nourished by his Body and Blood. In our churches Christ enlightens us from the tabernacle. He assures us, "Do not be afraid, I am with you." The Body and Blood of Christ consoles us, nourishes us, and protects us. This mystery invites us to gratitude and joy and calls us to an awesome intimacy with God, who is eager to be our very nourishment. Let us ask the grace to be "Eucharist," that is, to share the goods we have, to allow God to pour out our lives for others, and to become persons whose lives radiate thanksgiving.

The Sorrowful Mysteries
The Passion of Jesus Christ

The Sorrowful Mysteries contemplate the last hours of Jesus' earthly life. A sign of love is to be present to the one who suffers. These mysteries allow us a "you-are-there" experience as we witness the depths of the Lord's love for us, even to his last breath.

THE FIRST SORROWFUL MYSTERY

Jesus Prays in the Garden of Gethsemane

They went to a place called Gethsemane; and he said... "I am deeply grieved, even to death; remain here, and keep awake." And going a little farther, he threw himself on the ground and prayed that, if it were possible, the hour might pass from him. He said,

"Abba, Father, for you all things are possible; remove this cup from me; yet, not what I want, but what you want" (Mk 14:32, 34–36). *[H]is sweat became like great drops of blood falling down on the ground (Lk 22:44).*

Whoever experiences intense depression and oppressive sadness can feel Jesus' pain as he begged his Father to free him from his passion. The Father did not magically release his Son from the sufferings that awaited him. In his darkest hour, Jesus turned to God the Father with the confidence of a child, calling him "Abba," or Daddy. Traumatic life changes and losses can result in anxiety and sadness. At such stressful times, we can relate to Jesus' intense bloody sweat. Jesus heard no response, no *yes* for an answer. He only knew with clarity that the Father's will lay ahead. Let us allow Jesus to live in us, so that in our turn, we too can say, *"Father, not my will, but yours be done"* (cf. Mk 14:36).

The Second Sorrowful Mystery

The Scourging of Jesus

Then Pilate took Jesus and had him flogged (Jn 19:1).

When he spoke of his passion, Christ foretold the scourging (Mk 10:34; Mt 20:19; Lk 18:33). Jesus fully realized the meaning of the sentence of scourging. This punishment was reserved for runaway slaves and death-row criminals. The scourges furrowed deep wounds on Jesus' flesh. Jesus accepted the scourging as

atonement for all the sins committed through our senses, especially through touch. Sometimes one's skin is supersensitive; the touch of others brings pain instead of solace. Depression or mental illness and anxiety may bring on a cycle of physical, emotional, and mental anguish. Let us ask the grace to treat our bodies, as they are "temples of the Holy Spirit," with great respect, and to always honor Jesus' presence in others.

THE THIRD SORROWFUL MYSTERY

Jesus Is Mocked and Crowned with Thorns

Then the soldiers of the governor took Jesus into the governor's headquarters, and they gathered the whole cohort around him. They stripped him and put a scarlet robe on him, and after twisting some thorns into a crown, they put it on his head. They put a reed in his right hand and knelt before him and mocked him, saying, "Hail, King of the Jews!" They spat on him, and took the reed and struck him on the head (Mt 27:27–30).

The soldiers held Jesus in contempt—a presumed nobody setting himself up as a king. They thought it a laughing matter. In their cruelty they heaped insults and spittle on Jesus, the real King of Creation. Here Jesus endured the sufferings that many of the mentally ill or anxious endure: pain, humiliation, scorn, misunderstanding, and embarrassment. All during this time, Jesus was a prisoner. How often the acutely mentally ill are held captive, confined in asylums, incarcerated, or ostracized. While meditating this mystery, let us pray for the imprisoned and the mentally ill who receive cruel treatment from the unskilled or the seemingly uncaring, and for all who bear the crown of thorns of acute mental disorder.

The Fourth Sorrowful Mystery
Jesus Carries the Cross to Calvary

After mocking him, they stripped him of the robe and put his own clothes on him. Then they led him away to crucify him (Mt 27:31).

Jesus shouldered the cross alone. The abandonment he felt in the Garden of Gethsemane was even more intense as he went out bearing the cross alone. How often the mentally ill cry out, "You don't know me. You can't understand what it's like." When Peter denied Jesus, he said: "I do not *know* him" (Lk 22:57). Jesus wept over Jerusalem and said: "You did not *know* me" (see Lk 19:41–44). Now as he carries the cross for our sins, he is the *Great Unknown*. As he struggles under the weight of the cross, he bears the loneliness, the misunderstanding, the darkness of those suffering from depression, anxiety, addictions, and other forms of mental illness. In this mystery, let us ask the grace to know Jesus better in order to alleviate his suffering in those around us who are suffering in mind or in body.

The Crucifixion and Death of Jesus

When they came to the place that is called The Skull, they crucified Jesus there with the criminals, one on his right and one on his left. Then Jesus said, "Father, forgive them; for they do not know what they are doing." …Then Jesus, crying with a loud voice, said, "Father, into your hands I commend my spirit." Having said this, he breathed his last (Lk 23:33–34, 46).

On the cross, Jesus was drowned in an ocean of pain. Wave after wave of agony enveloped him. Yet, he forced himself to speak words of forgiveness and concern for his mother and disciples. He also cried out from thirst that tortured him both physically and mentally. Then he prayed: "My God, my God, why have you forsaken me?" (Mt 27:46; and the first words of Ps 22). Jesus' enemies mocked him as powerless to "come down from the cross" (Mt 27:40). Mental or emotional disorders often make one feel both abandoned and powerless. Others seem to stand away from us, just as the disciples hid lest others associate them with the man on the cross. In this mystery of Jesus' crucifixion, let us pray to unite our troubled emotions with the suffering Jesus, so that we may complete "what is lacking in Christ's afflictions" (see Col 1:24), as Saint Paul did.

The Glorious Mysteries
The Splendor of the Resurrected Lord

The Glorious Mysteries invite us to focus our attention on the majesty and power of the risen Lord. As the Bible says, "There is cause for rejoicing here" (See 2 Cor 4:15ff.). When all seems lost, these mysteries give us eternal reasons for hope.

THE FIRST GLORIOUS MYSTERY

The Resurrection

> *"Why do you look for the living among the dead?" (Lk 24:5)*

By his resurrection Jesus shows that he is truly God. The risen Jesus approached the disciples, Mary Magdalene, and the apostles on several occasions. When he first drew near, they did not know who he was. Then the tenderness and the familiarity of his voice struck a cord in those who saw him. At that moment they were delighted to see Jesus. Their ears once again recognized the tone of his voice. In this mystery, let us pray to recognize Jesus' presence and to hear his voice in the word of God and in the persons we meet.

The Ascension of Jesus into Heaven

While he was blessing them, he withdrew from them and was carried up into heaven (Lk 24:51).

Before Jesus was taken up into heaven, he issued the Great Commission—that is, the mandate to "go...and make disciples of all nations" (Mt 28:19). People who suffer mental illness may think themselves unlikely candidates for the work of evangelization. Yet, many who suffer anxiety, depression, PTSD, and unipolar and bipolar disorders are deeply involved in spreading the Gospel. In this mystery, let us pray for all missionaries. Ask the grace to be a missionary of God's peace and Good News by offering a smile instead of a frown, a compliment in place of a criticism, and a cheerful attitude despite the setbacks of the day.

THE THIRD GLORIOUS MYSTERY

The Holy Spirit Descends on the Apostles

When the day of Pentecost had come, they were all together in one place. And suddenly from heaven there came a sound like the rush of a violent wind, and it filled the entire house where they were sitting. Divided tongues, as of fire, appeared among them, and a tongue rested on each of them. All of them were filled with the Holy Spirit and began to speak in other languages, as the Spirit gave them ability (Acts 2:1–4).

Only the Holy Spirit gives us the grace to pray and open ourselves to the love of the Father and Son for us. The gifts of the Spirit include wisdom and fortitude. Let us ask these gifts for ourselves first of all. May the Spirit give us wisdom to seek the help and counsel that we need, and the fortitude and courage to be strong in accepting our weaknesses and sufferings.

THE FOURTH GLORIOUS MYSTERY

The Assumption

> [F]or the Mighty One has done great things for me,
>   and holy is his name (Lk 1:49).

Imagine how peaceful and loving was Mary's death. Jesus came for his Mother to reward her fidelity. We pray that at the hour of our death, Mary, our loving Mother, will be with us to console and guide us. May she assist us in the daily dying that is asked of us as we struggle through illness and weakness.

THE FIFTH GLORIOUS MYSTERY

The Coronation of Mary

> He has brought down the powerful from their thrones,
>   and lifted up the lowly (Lk 1:52).

Jesus, Mary's Son, rewarded his Mother's humility and fidelity. She who called herself God's handmaid was indeed exalted. Mary became Queen of heaven and earth and Mother of mercy.

We ask Mary, our Queen, to intercede for us so we can patiently accept the pain and anxiety of our situation in a spirit of faith and love.

The Rosary concludes with the Hail Holy Queen (see p. 85) and the following prayer:

Pray for us, O holy Mother of God
That we may be made worthy of the promises of Christ.

Let us pray. O God, whose only begotten Son, by his life, death, and resurrection has purchased for us the rewards of eternal life, grant, we beseech you, that meditating upon the mysteries of the most holy Rosary of the Blessed Virgin Mary, we may imitate what they contain and obtain what they promise, through the same Christ our Lord. Amen.

A Prayer to Mary
Who Unties the Knots of Our Lives

Near Ingolstodt, Germany, there is a small church with a painting of the Blessed Virgin Mary, Untier of Knots. The image shows our Lady untying the knots on a long ribbon. The original ribbon was from a wedding ceremony. A couple on the verge of divorce sought help from Mary. She untied the knots of what seemed unsolvable problems. Today Mary is honored under this title especially in Argentina, as well as in Europe and North America.[4]

Holy Mary, full of the presence of God, during your life you accepted with great humility the holy will of the Father and the legacy of your Son, our Lord Jesus Christ, and evil never entangled you with its deceptions. Since then you have interceded for all of our difficulties as you did at the wedding feast of Cana. With all simplicity and with patience, you have given us an example of how to untangle the knots in our complicated lives. By being our Mother forever, you arrange and make clear the path that unites us to our Lord.

Holy Mary, Mother of God and ours, with your maternal heart, untie the knots that upset our lives. We ask you to receive into your hands (*here mention your prayer request*) and deliver us from the chains and confusion that restrain us. Blessed Virgin Mary, through your grace, your intercession, and by your example, deliver us from evil, and untie the knots that keep us from

being united to God, so that free of all confusion and error, we may find him in all things, keep him in our hearts, and serve him always in our brothers and sisters. Amen.

To the Merciful Mother of the Mentally Ill

This author's son has been in state facilities more than forty years. He is often restrained and has suffered physically because of his illness.[5]

Sweet and lovely Lady
Who came to Tepeyac Hill
Put your arms around me
For I am mentally ill.
Shield me and protect me
From fear, anxiety and pain;
For my illness will not let me
Rejoice and know the gain.
Sweet and lovely lady
Full of grace, so heavenly
Put your arms around me
And hold me tenderly.
For you, my hope, are always near
Speak the words I need to hear:
"Oh, my child, be calm, be still.
I am your merciful Mother,
Mother of the mentally ill."

To Mary, Star of the Sea

Life often seems as chaotic as the motion of a boat being tossed about by rough seas. The Blessed Mother has been invoked for centuries by mariners as their Star—a steady beam of light leading to her Son, Jesus.

Dear Mary, Mother of Jesus and our Mother too, I come to you and beg you to intercede for me and all my family. As a star, which guides mariners on the sea, you direct all of us pilgrims on the way to the Father's house. Mary, Star of Evangelization, Star of the Sea, and Star of my life, guide me to a deeper union with your Son, Jesus, and to a joy that no one can take away. As you pointed the way to your Son, may my life be a star leading others to Jesus. May I keep my gaze fixed on your example, and may I please your Son, our Lord Jesus Christ. Amen.

Saintly Intercessors

A Litany for Help from the Saints

Mary, Mother of Jesus, you experienced the generosity of God in the graces you received. Assist me, so I can be alert to God's marvelous gifts to me.

Holy Mary, Mother of God, you experienced what it means
to be rejected and misunderstood.
Help me to trust that God fully understands and accepts me.

Quiet Joseph, spouse of Mary, you provided for
the Holy Family.
Provide for my spiritual, financial, and health needs.

Saint Peter, you were outspoken in your love for Jesus.
Teach me to speak and act so as to please Jesus.

Saint Andrew the Apostle, you were skilled at introducing
others to Christ.
*Give me ease in sharing my faith, so I can introduce others
to Jesus.*

Saint Paul, you were able to say, "It is no longer I who live, but Christ lives in me!"

Help me to live in a way that allows Christ to dwell in me.

Saint John Chrysostom, you preached well on how to live a practical Christian life.

Pray for me so I will know how to practice the Gospel in my life.

Saint Francis of Assisi, you saw God's reflection in all of creation.

Teach me to take joy in God's handiwork around me.

Saint Thomas Aquinas, your writings delved into the mystery of God.

Give me a love for the study of our faith.

Saint Thomas More, husband, father, lawyer, and martyr, you cheerfully gave your life for the faith.

Teach me cheerful fidelity in my daily life, so I too may be a saint one day.

Saint Teresa of Avila, you were most practical and yet a master of the interior life.

Teach me to grow in holiness as I go about my daily work.

Saint Philip Neri, you were a saint with a happy heart and a sense of humor.

Pray that I may never allow discouraging thoughts to steal my smile.

Saint Elizabeth Seton, you were a caring woman—wife, mother, widow, and foundress of the Sisters of Charity.

Teach me to practice charity at home, with my family, and with all whom I associate.

Saint Peter Julian Eymard, you gathered adorers around Jesus in the Eucharist.

Teach me a greater appreciation of Christ's real presence in the Eucharist.

Blessed André Bessette, your goodness and humility brought thousands to pray and provide for others.

Teach me trust in Divine Providence.

Saint Thérèse of Lisieux, you showed us how to reach heaven by your "little way."

Teach me to treasure every little opportunity to love God that comes my way.

Saint John Neumann, you left your homeland to serve among the immigrants in America.

Teach me to respect and love all immigrants.

Saint Edith Stein, you were a university professor, a philosopher, and a martyr.

Teach me to love holy wisdom.

Blessed Pier Giorgio Frassatti, you loved mountain climbing, parties, and the company of your friends. You focused your

studies so you could alleviate the burdens of the poor.
Teach me a just concern for my family and friends.

Saint Pio of Pietrelcina, you suffered the wounds of Christ and spent your life in humility and prayer.
Teach me patience in my trials and great compassion for those who suffer.

Blessed Teresa of Calcutta, you saw Christ in the poor.
Teach me generosity with the poor.

Blessed James Alberione, apostle of the media, you spent your life to preach the Gospel with the communications media.
Teach me to value the electronic media to bring me closer to God.

Blessed Timothy Giaccardo, you were an ardent devotee of the Eucharist as well as an apostle of the modern media.
Pray for all Christian writers, that they may be inspired by Jesus in the Eucharist.

Saint Gianna Molla, you were a wife and working mother.
Teach me to balance all my duties with joy and a spirit of prayer.

Saint Katharine Drexel, you were a wealthy woman who spent all your resources to educate and evangelize America's poorest.
Help me to be sensitive and caring to all in need.

Patron Saints for the
Anxious and Troubled Person

Saint Dymphna

Saint Dymphna died at the hands of her father, a nonbeliever who was violent and mentally ill. Angered that his daughter would not marry him, he pursued Dymphna from Ireland to Belgium, where he killed her. Dymphna's heroic martyrdom was around the year 600.

For centuries pilgrims have honored Dymphna at a shrine in the village of Gheel in the province of Antwerp, Belgium. From the thirteenth century, the people of Gheel have cared for persons afflicted with mental illness. In North America, pilgrims visit the Shrine of Saint Dymphna in Massillon, Ohio. Her feast day is celebrated on May 15.

Prayers for the Intercession of Saint Dymphna

Dearest Saint Dymphna, great wonder-worker for every affliction of mind and body, I humbly implore your powerful intercession with Jesus through Mary, Health of the Sick. You are filled with love and compassion for the thousands of patients brought to your shrine and for those who cannot come to your shrine, but invoke you in their own homes or hospitals. Show the same love and compassion toward me. The many miracles and

cures which have been wrought through your intercession give me great confidence that you will help me in my present illness (*here mention it*).

Good Saint Dymphna, the fervent faith and devotion of so many others who are afflicted with the same illness as I am inspire me to entrust myself to your special care. I trust in you and am absolutely confident of obtaining my urgent request, if it is for the greater glory of God and the good of my soul.

Saint Dymphna, young and beautiful, innocent and pure, help me to imitate your love of your purity. Give me the same strength and courage to withstand the temptations of the world, the flesh, and the devil. Help me to love God with my whole heart and serve him faithfully. As you bore the persecution of your father and the sufferings of an exile, obtain for me the patience I need to accept the cross of my illness and every other trial with loving resignation to God's will.

Saint Dymphna, through your glorious martyrdom for the love of Christ, help me to be loyal to my faith and my God as long as I live. And when the hour of my own death comes, stand at my side and pray for me that I may merit the eternal crown of glory in God's kingdom.

Good Saint Dymphna, I beg you to recommend my request to Mary, Health of the Sick and Comforter of the Afflicted, and to present it to Jesus, the Divine Physician.

Saint Dymphna, patroness of those who suffer distress of mind, beloved child of Jesus and Mary, pray for me and grant my request. *(Three times.)*

Our Father, Hail Mary, Glory be…

Saint Dymphna, virgin and martyr, pray for us.

Saint Benedict Joseph Labré

Benedict Joseph Labré (1748–1783) came from a devout and well-to-do French family. He learned to love the Scriptures from his uncle, a priest. Benedict attempted to enter several monasteries. Each time he was painfully afflicted with the deepest depression. During his final attempt to enter a monastery, Benedict became so ill that the monks kept him in the infirmary for two months before they sent him on his way. Once Benedict accepted his state and calling to be a lay wanderer for God, he became more sociable and caring toward other homeless people, even giving away food meant for him. Benedict lived his final years as a pilgrim, traveling on foot to Europe's religious shrines and spending hours in prayer before Jesus in the Blessed Sacrament. He had a remarkable devotion to the Forty Hours veneration of Jesus in the Eucharist. When Benedict died during Holy Week of 1783, the people of Rome proclaimed that "Il Santo"—the Saint—had died. Crowds poured into the church where Benedict's body lay to see the holy man. So many people flocked to see the remains of the poor wanderer for Christ that Holy Week services could not be held in the church where his body lay.

Men and women afflicted with mental and emotional disorders find a patron and intercessor in Saint Benedict. Along with the pain of severe mental illness, he lived a life of true holiness. His feast day is celebrated on April 16. The following prayer is attributed to Saint Benedict Joseph.

Eternal Father, through the Blood of Jesus, have mercy. Console us in the moment of need and tribulation, as you consoled Job, Hannah, and Tobias in their afflictions. Mary, Consoler of the Afflicted, pray to God that we may receive the grace for which we humbly pray. Amen.

A Litany of Saint Benedict Joseph Labré

Lord, *have mercy on us.*
Christ, *have mercy on us.*
Lord, *have mercy on us.*
God the Father of Heaven, *have mercy on us.*
God the Son, Redeemer of the world, *have mercy on us.*
God, the Holy Spirit, *have mercy on us.*

Holy Mary, Virgin Mother of God, *pray for us.*
Holy Mary, Glory of Loreto, *pray for us.*
Saint Benedict Joseph, beggar for Christ, *pray for us.*
Saint Benedict Joseph, despised by the world, *pray for us.*
Saint Benedict Joseph, renouncing earthly ties, *pray for us.*
Saint Benedict Joseph, reproaching our pride, *pray for us.*

Saint Benedict Joseph, tender to the outcast, *pray for us.*
Saint Benedict Joseph, ministering in charity hospitals, *pray for us.*
Saint Benedict Joseph, worker of mercy, *pray for us.*
Saint Benedict Joseph, saintly brother of the road, *pray for us.*
Saint Benedict Joseph, self-effacing unto death, *pray for us.*
Saint Benedict Joseph, example of humility, *pray for us.*
Saint Benedict Joseph, armor of chastity, *pray for us.*
Saint Benedict Joseph, zealous for souls, *pray for us.*
Saint Benedict Joseph, clean of heart, *pray for us.*
Saint Benedict Joseph, strength of the poor, *pray for us.*
Saint Benedict Joseph, example of Christ, *pray for us.*
Saint Benedict Joseph, who lived in holy poverty, *pray for us.*
Saint Benedict Joseph, childlike before God, *pray for us.*
Saint Benedict Joseph, holy wayfarer, *pray for us.*
Saint Benedict Joseph, leading us to Christ, *pray for us.*

Lamb of God, who takes away the sins of the world,
    spare us, O Lord.
Lamb of God, who takes away the sins of the world,
    graciously hear us, O Lord.
Lamb of God, who takes away the sins of the world,
    have mercy on us.

Let us pray.
Saint Benedict Joseph, beloved of God, lead us, poor travelers
on this earth, along the pilgrim way to God. Shield us from all

occasions of lust and pride that we may wear the garment of humility in the sight of our Lord Jesus Christ, and that we may be received into his everlasting kingdom.

Merciful Jesus, who by the life of your servant Benedict Joseph show your love for the very least of this world, grant us, we beseech you, those requests which the Holy Mendicant asks in our behalf, knowing that he desires to obtain for us only those things that would lead us to you, through your holy poverty on earth and your divine labors. Amen![6]

Words to Live By

God Rewards Humility

Humility comes from the Latin word "humus," *which means earth. The virtue of humility grounds us in our down-to-earth reality. It recognizes God's grandeur and power at work in our lives. Humility admits our good qualities and sees them as they truly are—gifts of God's loving providence accompanying our best efforts.*

[F]or he saves the humble. (Job 22:29)

Good and upright is the LORD;
   therefore he instructs sinners in the way.
He leads the humble in what is right,
   and teaches the humble his way. (Ps 25:8–9)

We are challenged to become childlike, not childish. Jesus points out the humility of children. Their natural simplicity and total trust in guardians are virtues worthy of heaven.

"Truly I tell you, unless you change and become like children, you will never enter the kingdom of heaven. Whoever becomes humble like this child is the greatest in the kingdom of heaven." (Mt 18:3–4)

A Right Self-Esteem

Because God loves each of us into existence, we are God's very own, and thus worthy of esteem.

My child, honor yourself with humility,
   and give yourself the esteem you deserve. (Sir 10:28)

On Medicine and Physicians

Old Testament writers directed, "Honor the physician." Saint Paul mentions the gift of healing in his First Letter to the Corinthians. Let us recommend our medical personnel—psychologists, psychiatrists, counselors, nurses—who share their knowledge and healing skill, to the loving care of Jesus the Divine Physician.

Honor physicians for their services,
   for the Lord created them;
for their gift of healing comes from the Most High....
The Lord created medicines out of the earth,

and the sensible will not despise them....
And he gave skill to human beings
  that he might be glorified in his marvelous works.
By them the physician heals and takes away pain;
  the pharmacist makes a mixture from them.
God's works will never be finished;
  and from him health spreads over all the earth....
Then give the physician his place, for the Lord created him;
  do not let him leave you, for you need him.
(Sir 38:1–2, 4, 6–8, 12)

Anger Management

We are to control our anger so it does not control us.

Unjust anger cannot be justified,
  for anger tips the scale to one's ruin.
Those who are patient stay calm until the right moment,
  and then cheerfulness comes back to them.
They hold back their words until the right moment;
  then the lips of many tell of their good sense....
For their conceit has led many astray,
  and wrong opinion has impaired their judgment.
(Sir 1:22–24, 3:24)

Think About These Things

When we catch ourselves brooding over real or imagined hurts, or find ourselves in the underground darkness of negativity, let us ask God to open the eyes of our heart to see the good things around us.

[W]hatever is true, whatever is honorable, whatever is just, whatever is pure, whatever is pleasing, whatever is commendable, if there is any excellence and if there is anything worthy of praise, think about these things. Keep on doing the things that you have learned and received and heard and seen in me, and the God of peace will be with you. (Phil 4:8–9)

About Heaven

Saint Francis of Assisi once said that "every pain is my delight, since it brings me closer to paradise." The thought of heaven encourages us.

"Do not store up for yourselves treasures on earth, where moth and rust consume and where thieves break in and steal; but store up for yourselves treasures in heaven, where neither moth nor rust consumes and where thieves do not break in and steal. For where your treasure is, there your heart will be also." (Mt 6:19–21)

Saint Paul was privileged to have a foretaste of heaven. Let's count on his words to prepare for heaven.

What no eye has seen, nor ear heard,
  nor the human heart conceived,
what God has prepared for those who love him. (1 Cor 2:9)

When we are having a dark day, or feel an oppressive mood gripping us, we can turn to the last pages of the Bible for a glimpse of the Light, who awaits us in heaven.

[T]he throne of God and of the Lamb will be in it, and his servants will worship him; they will see his face, and his name will be on their foreheads. And there will be no more night; they need no light of lamp or sun, for the Lord God will be their light, and they will reign forever and ever. (Rev 22:3–5)

A Hymn to Love

In his First Letter to the Corinthians, Saint Paul explained the meaning of charity, or true love. Spiritual writers say that after reading this portion of First Corinthians, it is well to re-read it, replacing the word "charity" with our own name, or simply with the pronoun "I." We might also pray

these words before going to bed, turning the sentences into a self-examina-
tion: "Have I been patient; have I been kind...?" Saint Paul reminds us
that charity—self-giving love—is the bottom line of Christian life. This is
the criterion that really counts:

If I speak in the tongues of mortals and of angels, but do not have love, I am a noisy gong or a clanging cymbal. And if I have prophetic powers, and understand all mysteries and all knowledge, and if I have all faith, so as to remove mountains, but do not have love, I am nothing. If I give away all my possessions, and if I hand over my body so that I may boast, but do not have love, I gain nothing.

Love is patient; love is kind; love is not envious or boastful or arrogant or rude. It does not insist on its own way; it is not irritable or resentful; it does not rejoice in wrongdoing, but rejoices in the truth. It bears all things, believes all things, hopes all things, endures all things.

Love never ends. But as for prophecies, they will come to an end; as for tongues, they will cease; as for knowledge, it will come to an end. For we know only in part, and we prophesy only in part; but when the complete comes, the partial will come to an end. When I was a child, I spoke like a child, I thought like a child, I reasoned like a child; when I became an adult, I put an end to childish ways. For now we see in a mirror, dimly, but then we will see face to face. Now I know only in part; then I will know fully, even as I have been fully known. And now faith, hope, and love abide, these three; and the greatest of these is love. (1 Cor 13:1–13)

The Armor of God

Some describe our day-to-day struggle to follow God's will as a spiritual combat. Here Saint Paul exhorts us to put on God's body armor—the spiritual equivalent of a "bulletproof vest" for the soul.

[B]e strong in the Lord and in the strength of his power. Put on the whole armor of God, so that you may be able to stand against the wiles of the devil. For our struggle is not against enemies of blood and flesh, but against the rulers, against the authorities, against the cosmic powers of this present darkness, against the spiritual forces of evil in the heavenly places. Therefore, take up the whole armor of God, so that you may be able to withstand on that evil day, and having done everything, to stand firm. Stand therefore, and fasten the belt of truth around your waist, and put on the breastplate of righteousness.

As shoes for your feet put on whatever will make you ready to proclaim the Gospel of peace. With all of these, take the shield of faith, with which you will be able to quench all the flaming arrows of the evil one. Take the helmet of salvation, and the sword of the Spirit, which is the word of God. (Eph 6:10–17)

Our Ultimate Goal

Saint Paul reminds us that "the one thing necessary" is not a thing, but the loving Person of Jesus Christ who desires to be one with us.

[I]t is no longer I who live, but it is Christ who lives in me.... My little children, for whom I am again in the pain of childbirth until Christ is formed in you! (Gal 2:20; 4:19)

Short Gospel Prayers

"Gospel" comes from old English "Godspell," meaning good news. The four Christian Gospels of Matthew, Mark, Luke, and John, each in its own way, bring God's Good News to us. Saint Luke's is especially a Gospel of joy. The evangelists Matthew, Mark, and John also speak of joy and happiness or blessedness. Heeding their message brings deep joy. Let us pray with these words of the Gospel.

"Lord, teach us to pray." (Lk 11:1)

"Master, Master, we are perishing!" (Lk 8:24)

"Lord, if you choose, you can make me clean!" (Lk 5:12)

"I believe; help my unbelief!" (Mk 9:24)

"Jesus, Son of David, have mercy on me!" (Lk 18:38)

"Father, I have sinned against heaven and before you. I am no longer worthy to be called your son." (Lk 15:21)

"Lord, let me see again." (Lk 18:41)

"Lord, let our eyes be opened." (Mt 20:33)

"[Lord], give us this bread always." (Jn 6:34)

"Master, we have worked all night long but have caught nothing. Yet if you say so, I will let down the nets." (Lk 5:5)

"Lord, to whom can we go? You have the words of eternal life. We have come to believe and know that you are the Holy One of God." (Jn 6:68–69)

"[Lord], give me this water, so that I may never be thirsty." (Jn 4:15)

"Stay with us." (Lk 24:29)

"Yes, Lord, I believe that you are the Messiah, the Son of God." (Jn 11:27)

Resources for Personal Growth

Cook, Marshall J., *How to Handle Worry: A Catholic Approach* (revised edition). Boston: Pauline Books & Media, 2007.

————. *The How to Handle Worry Workbook: A Catholic Approach.* Boston: Pauline Books & Media, 2007.

Has anxiety disrupted your serenity? Marshall Cook develops a practical approach to deal with the worries and anxieties that creep into our lives. With humor and insight, he offers useful suggestions that help to put worry in a faith perspective. Bringing our burdens to God can ease the tension and lead to greater peace of mind.

Frankl, Victor. *Man's Search for Meaning.* New York: Simon and Schuster Pocket Books, 1985.

Doctor Frankl spent most of World War II as a prisoner in a Nazi concentration camp. His vivid yet serene description of life in the camp shows how he reached the conclusion that a person "who has a why in life can live with any how." Victor Frankl's reflections led him to practice a kindly form of reality therapy. His book is therapeutic in itself.

Groeschel, Benedict. *Arise from Darkness: What to Do When Life Doesn't Make Sense.* San Francisco: Ignatius Press, 1995.

In this volume Father Groeschel offers advice to overcome sadness. Prayers from various sources are at the end of every chapter. One chapter describes how the author dealt with the suicide of one of his charges. He concludes the chapter with prayers for those who die from suicide.

—————. *The Courage to Be Chaste.* New York: Paulist Press, 1985.

This book is addressed to all who want to live a chaste life, including persons with a same-sex attraction.

—————. *Grace and Personal Change.* New York: Alba House, 2001.

In this 58-minute audio presentation, Groeschel uses powerful stories to show how addictions, lifestyles, and other crippling anxieties can stop our spiritual growth or, with the merciful grace of God, can lead to greater faith and change.

—————. *Knowing the Father: Understanding the Depths of Love and Mercy That Embrace Us.* New York: Alba House, 2001.

In this series of seven CDs or cassettes, Groeschel leads the listener to a deeper understanding of God's tender mercies toward us right until the moment of death.

—————. *Listening At Prayer.* New York: Paulist Press, 1984.

This is an easy-to-read explanation of how to pray with a heart open to God. The author also gives tips for praying with the psalms.

—————. *Saint Thérèse of Lisieux: Light and Darkness.* New York: Alba House, 1998.

Groeschel tells of a woman who loved and hoped, yet suffered from bad weather and was affected by long fasts and lack of sleep.

—————. *Stumbling Blocks and Stepping Stones: Spiritual Answers to Psychological Questions.* Mahwah, NJ: Paulist Press, 1987.

This book addresses those with heavy crosses to bear, including mental illness. The author also presents the story of St. Benedict Labré.

Hermes, Kathryn James, FSP. *Prayers for Surviving Depression*. Boston: Pauline Books & Media, 2004.

The author offers prayers drawn from a variety of sources to help those who suffer from depression.

———. *Surviving Depression: A Catholic Approach*. Boston: Pauline Books & Media, 2004.

After a stroke at age 23, the author suffered years of depression, sleep deprivation, and mood swings without realizing the cause of her problems. Through a correct diagnosis, much prayer, and reflection, she shares her experience in survival as a believer. This best-seller guides one to see Divine Providence shining through the darkness of our spiritual, emotional, and mental states.

Kelsey, Morton T. *Christo-Psychology*. New York: Crossroad, 1988.

This book is principally concerned with psychology, yet it offers some great insights into prayer under emotional duress, as well as help with dreams. Kelsey has authored several titles on spirituality and psychology; for the most part, these titles are for the caregivers rather than the mentally ill.

Larrañaga, Ignacio. *Sensing Your Hidden Presence*. Sherbrooke, Canada: Médiaspaul, 1992.

A compelling book on practical means of praying better. Larrañaga is a psychologist as well as an internationally-known retreat director and popular spiritual writer.

The Complete Parallel Bible with the Apocryphal/Deuterocanonical Books. New York: Oxford University Press, 1993.

Side-by-side translations of the New Revised Standard Version, *the* Revised English Bible, *the* New American Bible, *and the* New

Jerusalem Bible. *The slight variations in the translations help the reader to meditate Bible passages in a relaxed and prayerful way.*

Moesteller, Sue. *A Place to Hold My Shaky Heart: Reflections from Life in Community.* New York: Crossroad Publishing, 1998.
Moesteller gives precious insights from living with formerly homeless people, some mentally troubled, others mentally challenged.

Soukup, Paul, SJ. *Out of Eden: 7 Ways God Restores Blocked Communication.* Boston: Pauline Books & Media, 2006.
In the Garden of Eden, Adam and Eve succumbed to fear and cut off their communication with God. The tempter of Eden still disturbs us today, persuading us to doubt ourselves, to overvalue possessions and appearance, to brood over the past, to seek revenge. Yet there is a way out. God himself restores our blocked communication, helping us to heal our relationships and lead lives of deeper connection and meaning.

Udris, John. *Holy Daring: The Fearless Trust of Thérèse of Lisieux.* Boston: Pauline Books & Media, 2007.
A Carmelite nun who died at the age of twenty-four, Saint Thérèse had an extraordinary confidence in the goodness and boundless love of God. Despite the darkness and uncertainty she herself experienced, she believed that God can be absolutely trusted. Her example encourages us when it seems impossible to surrender our lives to God.

Wicks, Robert. *Clinical Handbook of Pastoral Counseling.* Mahwah, NJ: Paulist Press, 1985.
A detailed manual for those engaged in the ministry of caring for the troubled in spirit.

————. *Snow Falling on Snow: Themes from the Spiritual Landscape.* Mahwah, NJ: Paulist Press, 2001.

Readable and inspirational work.

————. *Riding the Dragon: 10 Lessons for Inner Strength in Challenging Times.* Mahwah, NJ: Paulist Press, 2004 and 2005.

Also available in audio format from Saint Anthony Messenger Press, Cincinnati. Wicks draws on his own experience, as well as on Christian and Eastern spiritual wisdom to guide and encourage his readers. He suggests "riding the dragons" of our darkness and using them to grow rather than grovel in negativity. The author's practical advice, enlivened with stories, shows the reader how he applies his own lessons.

Notes

1. Excerpt from Letter "To Louise Abbot" (1959) from *The Habit of Being: The Letters of Flannery O'Connor,* edited by Sally Fitzgerald. Copyright © 1979 by Regina O'Connor. Reprinted by permission of Farrar, Straus and Giroux, LLC (North American permission) and by permission of Harold Matson Co., Inc. on behalf of the Mary Flannery O'Connor Charitable Trust (worldwide permission excluding North America).

2. This prayer was composed by Father Gabriele Amorth, SSP. Excerpted from "Prayer for Inner Healing" from *An Exorcist Tells His Story.* Copyright © 1999 Ignatius Press. Used with permission.

3. This prayer was composed by Father Gabriele Amorth, SSP. Excerpted from "Prayer for Deliverance" from *An Exorcist Tells His Story.* Copyright © 1999 Ignatius Press. Used with permission.

4. The prayer of Our Lady Untier of Knots © Mario H. Ibertis Rivera. www.desatadora.com.ar

5. "To the Merciful Mother of the Mentally Ill." This prayer was composed by Mrs. Mildred Duff, cofoundress of the Guild of St. Benedict Labré.

6. From the Guild of St. Benedict Labré, Box 200, Buzzard's Bay, MA 02532.

SISTER MARY PETER MARTIN is a native of Youngstown, Ohio. After becoming a Daughter of St. Paul, she worked as a media evangelizer in several areas, including New York, Alaska, and Hawaii. She holds a master's in education from Boston College. From 2003 to 2004, she participated in an intense academic year of study on the roots of the Pauline Family, religious life, Church history, and spirituality. For ten years she served on the board of directors of a national Catholic evangelization organization. She currently resides in Toronto, where she continues her work in media evangelization and in the formation of Pauline Cooperators.

BOOKS & MEDIA

The Daughters of St. Paul operate book and media centers at the following addresses. Visit, call or write the one nearest you today, or find us on the World Wide Web, www.pauline.org

CALIFORNIA
3908 Sepulveda Blvd, Culver City, CA 90230 — 310-397-8676
2640 Broadway Street, Redwood City, CA 94063 — 650-369-4230
5945 Balboa Avenue, San Diego, CA 92111 — 858-565-9181

FLORIDA
145 S.W. 107th Avenue, Miami, FL 33174 — 305-559-6715

HAWAII
1143 Bishop Street, Honolulu, HI 96813 — 808-521-2731
Neighbor Islands call: — 866-521-2731

ILLINOIS
172 North Michigan Avenue, Chicago, IL 60601 — 312-346-4228

LOUISIANA
4403 Veterans Memorial Blvd, Metairie, LA 70006 — 504-887-7631

MASSACHUSETTS
885 Providence Hwy, Dedham, MA 02026 — 781-326-5385

MISSOURI
9804 Watson Road, St. Louis, MO 63126 — 314-965-3512

NEW JERSEY
561 U.S. Route 1, Wick Plaza, Edison, NJ 08817 — 732-572-1200

NEW YORK
150 East 52nd Street, New York, NY 10022 — 212-754-1110

PENNSYLVANIA
9171-A Roosevelt Blvd, Philadelphia, PA 19114 — 215-676-9494

SOUTH CAROLINA
243 King Street, Charleston, SC 29401 — 843-577-0175

TENNESSEE
4811 Poplar Avenue, Memphis, TN 38117 — 901-761-2987

TEXAS
114 Main Plaza, San Antonio, TX 78205 — 210-224-8101

VIRGINIA
1025 King Street, Alexandria, VA 22314 — 703-549-3806

CANADA
3022 Dufferin Street, Toronto, ON M6B 3T5 — 416-781-9131

¡También somos su fuente para libros, videos y música en español!

Christ in everyday life

So that we may better serve your needs, please take a moment to complete this card. As a thank you, we'll send you a free booklet. All information will remain confidential. ***Thank you.***

Name:

Address:

City, State, Zip: _____ E-mail: _____

Age: ☐ 20-30   ☐ 31-40   ☐ 41-50   ☐ 51-60   ☐ Over 60   Gender: ☐ Female   ☐ Male

Title of book purchased:

Where do you purchase most of your books?
☐ General bookstore
☐ Pauline store
☐ Religious bookstore
☐ School/Parish
☐ Online
☐ Direct Mail/Catalog
☐ Other: _____

What subject areas do you purchase the most?
☐ Adult Faith
☐ Spirituality
☐ Prayer/Devotions
☐ Family
☐ Children
☐ Saints/Biographies
☐ Scripture
☐ Theology
☐ Teaching Resources
☐ Church Documents
☐ Mariology
☐ Faith & Culture
☐ Other: _____

How did you find out about this book?
☐ Word of mouth
☐ Newspaper/Book Review
☐ Internet
☐ Direct Mail/Catalog
☐ Browsing at store
☐ Other: _____

Would you like to receive online promotions from us? ☐ Yes ☐ No

Would you like to receive our complete catalog? ☐ Yes ☐ No

800-876-4463
www.pauline.org

BUSINESS REPLY MAIL

FIRST-CLASS MAIL   PERMIT NO. 5689   BOSTON MA

POSTAGE WILL BE PAID BY ADDRESSEE

ATTN MARKETING DEPARTMENT
PAULINE BOOKS & MEDIA
50 SAINT PAULS AVENUE
JAMAICA PLAIN MA 02130-9930

NO POSTAGE
NECESSARY
IF MAILED
IN THE
UNITED STATES